HER JOURNEY

HER JOURNEY

▼

Stories of Entrepreneurs

Darlene E. Jones M.Ed.

Writer's Showcase
San Jose New York Lincoln Shanghai

Her Journey
Stories of Entrepreneurs

Writer's Showcase
an imprint of iUniverse.com, Inc.

For information address:
iUniverse.com, Inc.
5220 S 16th, Ste. 200
Lincoln, NE 68512
www.iuniverse.com

ISBN: 0-595-16655-5

Printed in the United States of America

This book is dedicated to the four women who share their stories and in doing so, provide inspiration for those who wish to pursue their own dreams of running entrepreneurial ventures.

EPIGRAPH

▼

When I last spoke to each of these women, every one was still running their own business and making a profit. I salute each of them as they continue their respective journeys.

CONTENTS

▼

List of Illustrations

▼

LIST OF TABLES

▼

PREFACE

▼

Her Journey is a book about a phenomenon in the workforce that has caught the attention of many women in North America: entrepreneurship. For as many reasons as there are women who are becoming entrepreneurs, this practice currently enjoys a great deal of popularity. You may already be one of the many contributors to this way of doing business. Perhaps you are considering joining the ranks of the entrepreneur. Or maybe you are just curious about the reasons women seem drawn towards this idea of heading up their own businesses.

You will meet four women entrepreneurs. Although their names have been changed these are real women with real lives and real experiences. While each of their stories is different, similar patterns weave in and out of each of their tales as owner/operator of their own businesses. The warp and woof of their entrepreneurial lives creates an existence for each of them that can best be described as a metaphorical journey.

The use of the journey metaphor was a natural result of listening to these women recounting anecdotes about their lives as female entrepreneurs. For centuries we have used metaphors to tell stories, to create visual explanations. In *Her Journey* the metaphor of a journey describes entrepreneurship in terms of the patterns observed at the outset of the entrepreneurial journey, en route, and at the probable termination of the journey.

INTRODUCTION

▼

The initial stirrings for this book on the entrepreneurial journey arose from personal experience with such ventures throughout my own life. As a youngster I had my own paper route for seven years, which furnished me with an allowance that my parents could not provide. But more importantly to me over the years, I developed certain characteristics that money cannot buy. For example, persistence emerged as a trait that surfaced as I constantly canvassed the neighbourhood for additional customers. As a teenager, I continued my own entrepreneurial journey by exchanging the paper route for babysitting services. While I learned that good customer service generated repeat business, I also began to understand a need for self-satisfaction in choosing to work with specific clients.

As an adult, I combined an interest in education with an interest in the entrepreneurial venture as part of a staff that opened a private school. The challenge to provide excellent education for the students, while paying teachers' salaries, renting a facility, and incurring and paying additional expenses, was at times frustrating, yet very exhilarating.

After leaving the private school and subsequently completing my undergraduate degree, I continued to be drawn towards the entrepreneurial venture. I read new venture stories in magazines such as *Success* and *Entrepreneur*, and considered opening a full-time tutoring business. But an overwhelming desire to continue a journey in learning led to a return to school as a graduate student in education.

One of the graduate courses focused on female victimisation and male oppression through authors such as Carol Gilligan and Adrienne Rich. Depression set in as I wondered if there was any hope for the working female population. Yet at the same time, the media was filled with the efforts of famous new venturers such as fashion designer Donna Karan, lifestyle entrepreneur Martha Stewart, and Body Shop franchiser Anita Roddick. At this same time I met a local entrepreneur who was supporting her family. She encouraged me to accept freelance jobs, and to my amazement, I had to refuse work to continue with my courses. Optimism for the female entrepreneur at the dawn of the 21st century replaced my once disheartened spirit.

As a graduate student I decided to combine my interests in education, women, and entrepreneurship in an exploration of the female entrepreneur. Such an exploration made sense because a partnership had already been formed between business and education to prepare students for the work world. This work world included female entrepreneurs. High schools and colleges in the area were offering entrepreneurial studies to students who wanted to learn specifically about starting their own new ventures, not just about business in general. The educational world was becoming increasingly interested in the entrepreneurial world, and I was ready to add to our knowledge of this entrepreneurial phenomenon.

I wondered why entrepreneurship had grown at an unprecedented rate in North America in the final years of the 20th century. It did not take long to discover the answer to that basic question. Corporate downsizing and re-engineering had resulted in masses of laid off employees. For some of these former employees, entrepreneurship seemed to provide an alternative to employment in a shrinking job market. They began to create their own jobs. In the early 90s Hisrich and Peters told us "we are living in the age of the entrepreneur" in their book, *On Your Own: How To Start, Develop and Manage A New Business.* By 1996 *Canadian Business* reported that "small businesses and start-ups are the engine of the economy right now." In short, some of North America's workforce chose to journey into entrepreneurial ventures.

I set out to interview and observe four women entrepreneurs who were among these venturers. For me it was a method of deciding whether to eventually join this growing group of workers. But first I wanted to discover whether certain patterns exist in this popular phenomenon that may prove helpful to understand before embarking on such a journey. These women allowed me to observe them at their workplace in action. They discussed their work as an integral part of their lives as a whole. Each of them described the life of an entrepreneur not merely as a process, but as a journey filled with challenges and accomplishments. As certain patterns revealed themselves in each of these journeys, a specific, holistic combination of elements emerged that seemed crucial to the entrepreneurial experience.

This holistic grouping of major elements in the metaphorical journey of the entrepreneur is threefold. Personal elements such as skills, attitudes, personality traits, and sociological conditions tended to be in place before the journey was undertaken. Contextual elements referred to those aspects of the journey by which the women derived a sense of meaning about their entrepreneurial experience once it had begun. Operational elements designated the specific items pertaining to the running of the chosen business, and may in fact be the reason for terminating the journey. All three elements combine holistically to guide the entrepreneur on her journey.

Thus this three-pronged approach serves to advance our knowledge of entrepreneurs as we seek to understand the phenomenon of entrepreneurship in the new millennium. Those of you who may be reassessing your own business may use this book. Alternatively, those of you who are aspiring entrepreneurs considering the possibility of embarking upon such a venture may want to evaluate the elements more closely. Finally, this book is for anyone interested in simply learning more about the world of the female entrepreneur as it presents a snapshot of four North American women on their respective entrepreneurial journeys.

CHAPTER ONE

▼

CONNECTING WITH OTHERS IN HER JOURNEY: AMY, COFFEE SHOP FRANCHISEE

Amy leads a demanding lifestyle. With a staff of eleven young adults and a coffee shop franchise that must remain open to customers for sixteen hours a day, she rarely sleeps more than four hours a night. This owner/manager thrives on running her own establishment. But it is her 100% commitment to children, staff and family that ignites the passion for the venture of this "people person".

For eighteen months Amy has owned and operated a coffee shop franchise with an initial cost of nearly $400,000. "That doesn't include anything. That is just for the name." The franchiser opened one shop twenty-five years ago and has since established so many more that he can ask for, and get, a high buy-in price.

While Amy carries a large franchise name, she ultimately runs the shop by herself. In other words she is her own boss, which she enjoys immensely. However, she also recognizes that as sole owner/manager she ultimately must take full responsibility for the business. In addition to running the business, she takes her turn serving the customer "on line" for 36 to 40 hours a week. Furthermore, she spends at least 35 hours managing the books.

It took Amy seventeen years of working in the medical field as a nurse, and running clinics before she decided to put the same long hours into operating her own business. "I think I always knew I would do something [entrepreneurial]." She started researching the possibility when she was in her early thirties, but felt the time was not right while her children were young. She understood there would be a major time commitment in running her own business, so she waited until her children were in school before opening a shop.

When she bought the franchise she was married, but a year and a half later was separated from her husband. She is now on her own. Her concern is that the present coffee franchise will not sustain her for long. She gives her business three to six years before moving on because "economically it is not what it should be."

So far the shop is not particularly profitable, yet Amy remains. For Amy success is not entirely equated with the bottom line. "I think it is really important how you measure success. It is not always financial."

Her philosophy about money is that it is not an obstacle because borrowing money is part of the businessperson's life. "That's life. Get used to it or get out of it…I think when you are setting up a business you have to be sure you can deal with the financial end. And I don't mean that you have the money, but you can cope with the ups and downs." If you cannot deal with the ambiguity of owning one's business, then Amy says flat out "Don't take it on!"

Although she struggles sometimes with the lack of profits, Amy measures her success in something less tangible than money. Her personal focus is twofold. First she enjoys running her own business. She once laboured long hours for others. Now she extends her working days for her own establishment. While she may follow specific franchise guidelines, she has created further guidelines as the owner of her shop that she expects her employees to follow. When asked if she wants to be her own boss, she answers quickly and straightforwardly, "Yes I do!"

Second, Amy measures success in terms of her relationships with both employees and customers. "My staff knows pretty much everything that is happening in my life and I know a lot that happens in their lives." She sees herself as both a mom and a friend to her staff, much as she is to her own two children. As for her customers, she talks about them as part of her extended family too. Sometimes they discuss their families with Amy. Often they celebrate births, birthdays and anniversaries at her shop. "It is fun literally being part of people's lives…I didn't expect that." She wants to remain in business because the staff and customers are "like one really big family in here—and it is growing with the customers that come in."

It is 6:00 on a dark, cold January morning and Amy, already neatly dressed in her uniform, works alone behind the counter. Music from "Joseph and the Amazing Technicolour Dreamcoat" creates an upbeat, lively atmosphere. Her shop's faux-finished yellow walls and canvas paintings reflect the warmth of the lowered lighting. "I keep the lights turned down low because there are a number of walkers out this early in the morning and I don't want them thinking I am open for business yet." The franchise sets the hours so she must open at 7:00 a.m. and close at 11:00 p.m.

She rapidly measures coffee into coffee filters, giving each one a twist before placing it on the counter, ready for the large urns of "java" she will prepare later. With a quick dial she turns the dishwasher on, and then sets up five coffee urns in preparation for the early morning customers. She straightens tables and chairs, making sure the shop looks appealing. Her staff should have done this last night, but they have not been working up to their potential lately. She blames herself for having been too busy moving house during the Christmas season to be on top of things at the store. She tells me she plans to "crack down again."

Prior to opening the shop, Amy runs downstairs to her office to comb her hair and put on a little make up, ready to greet her customers. While downstairs she counts the milk containers stored in the downstairs refrigerator, before counting those in the shop's refrigerator. Today she must order her weekly supply of milk, which varies from week to week and season to season, so there is not an automatic count.

At precisely 7:00 am Amy unlocks the shop door. At 7:01 her first customer arrives, and asks whether Amy carries bagels. Amy apologises with, "Yes, but I'm sorry the delivery has not arrived yet." She suggests another place to try, but realises that shop received the same delivery, and again apologises to the woman.

When the second customer arrives, Amy greets her by name and asks, "How is the family?" They chat while Amy loses no time getting her coffee. It is a personal conversation, at the end of which Amy adds, "Don't forget your card." (Regular customers keep a card that allows them a free coffee for every five purchased.) "Do you have a busy day ahead of you?" She takes the time to listen to the answer before adding, "That's good. Take care."

She moves constantly. Now she empties the clean dishes from the dishwasher. She then proceeds to place fresh baked goods in baskets ready for the display case. The bakery delivers them daily before she arrives at work at 6:00 a.m. She tells me that she particularly dislikes having problems with this delivery because it means she has to come to work even earlier. As it is, she arises every morning early enough to walk her dog before driving the fifteen minutes to the shop to be here by 6:00. Today she is a little tired because she also waited up for her daughter to come in from babysitting at 2:00 a.m. to chat with her; Amy has had about two hours sleep.

While it is early and there are no customers in the shop Amy takes change from the cash register. "I'm just running next door for the newspapers." She dashes out the door, and returns somewhat flustered. "He wanted to chat and when I told him I was alone, it didn't seem to matter." Then she proceeds to fill me in on this man who is not the easiest neighbour. Apparently he came in one day when she was absent from the shop to accuse one of her staff members of damaging his property. "When I heard this, I went over and lambasted him for yelling at one of my staff members and told him to never do that again!" While she relates this incident to me, she pours a cup of coffee for this man and then delivers it to him. Upon her return she washes her hands, something she does frequently throughout the day.

A customer walks in who had left her dog tied up outside the shop. The Health Department allows dogs in the shop, as long as there are no complaints from other customers. Amy asks: "Do you want to bring your dog in and sit awhile?"

Another regular customer arrives and Amy immediately says, "Croissant–no butter." She then asks, "How is your throat S?" He replies and adds, "Keep the change." Amy responds, "No, no." He insists. She says, "We'll talk later!" Two of his co-workers walk in. Amy comments "You're early today. Where is B?" They order coffee and she asks, "Are you munching anything today?" Both order a muffin. They tell Amy that they will not be able to smoke outside today because of the freezing temperatures. Amy offers them the use of her employees' rooms downstairs if they wish to have a cigarette before going into work. "I'm sorry you can't smoke in my shop."

At 7:30 she pours herself a cup of coffee and sits down. Before she has time to take a sip, two more customers walk into the shop and she jumps up quickly to serve them.

Another woman walks in and orders coffee. As Amy pours her coffee, she asks, "How's the car doing?" They chat about the customer's car and cars in general. A gentleman walks in, and Amy involves him in the conversation by saying, "We're talking about cars." The woman leaves, saying, "Bye Amy. Enjoy your day!" The gentleman picks up his order and adds, "Have a great day Amy."

At 7:45 a.m. the first employee arrives. Jane, a biochemistry student, is quiet, but pleasant. She pours herself an orange juice and sits down. Amy joins her for a chat.

Jane was one of the first 17 Amy hired before the shop opened, before Amy knew whether she even had the shop. Out of a possible 2000 applications, Amy had narrowed the number of interviews to 300. "I basically made up my mind on a person within about 20 seconds. And the rest of the interview was absolutely useless." Each of the seventeen was told there was nothing definite, no starting date, no shop, only a cell phone number. Yet Amy had put together training binders, which she gave each one. "I'll let you know. We'll be in touch. Take your binder. Start your homework." Eventually Amy and the 17 students trained in a large metropolitan city for three intensive days, set up the shop and wrote two franchise exams. "And if they failed, they lost the job!" The day after their exams they opened the shop; everyone had passed and was certified. "That was for $6.85 an hour!"

As manager of her own establishment, Amy demands more from her staff than does the franchiser. "The franchise sets standards, and I agree with the standards…But I have a group of my own standards…you'll notice when they [her employees] are finished doing certain things, they immediately go wash their hands. If they don't then it is me on them. There are certain things that I want to see when I am in places and I expect them here. And there is no excuse. I don't care if you are making $6.00 or $60.00 an hour, you have to have morals. You have to have ethics. And you have to be a worker, and if you are not, you are not going to make more than $6.85 an hour ever."

Yet Amy supports her staff when it comes to customer complaints laid against any one of them. "I learned years ago if someone came in to complain about my staff and what they did or did not do I would apologise to the customer. I would say, 'I am very sorry. They are not usually like that. I'll speak to them. I will handle it.' But I would never go back to my staff and say, 'Why did you do that?' I would say, 'Tell me what happened?'

Because nine out of ten times it is not necessarily the staff and how they have dealt with something. It is the perception of the customer…At times it is the staff; it is me…You are tired. You have had a bad day."

Meanwhile, today seems to be a good day as she serves an elderly couple a muffin. Amy asks, "Do you want that cut in half, and would you like butter with either half?" She gives them an extra pat of butter "just in case". She places each half on a separate plate for them, and takes the coffee over to a table for them. She asks if they are chilly since the shop's inside door is open. Before they actually respond, Amy closes the door while chatting about the windy weather.

It is a dull drizzly morning outside at 8:30. Jane comments that more customers usually come to the shop when it is raining, but today there are fewer customers. Amy and Jane decide this is due to the season. Christmas is over, but Amy adds, "people are getting their bills from Christmas and are simply not spending money on coffee—not going out right now. The numbers were down last year at this time too." Jane and Amy recall that Amy fired an employee last year at this time, using the decreased numbers as an excuse for not needing her services. Amy indicates that she hates having to let someone go, or even having to cut hours for her staff because she knows they are counting on the money.

Amy sits sipping coffee, but feels guilty because she has not taken the bean inventory yet so she could call in the order. As the manager, Amy demands that her staff do the "bean count" prior to store opening. Since she does not expect her staff to do what she will not do, she walks to the counter to get on with the job of taking the bean inventory for the day.

Maintaining a good coffee bean inventory in a coffee shop keeps expenses high. While the coffee shop industry exploded in the 1990s, the price of the coffee beans remains expensive. Amy's inventory of beans costs her "somewhere between $7000 and $10000 a month–just in beans. That is expensive. They are not cheap." On top of the cost of the beans are the additional taxes levied. "The government is tough!"

In addition to inventory costs, Amy has other monthly expenses. First she pays exorbitant rent for her excellent location on the corner of the main street in a mid-sized city. Then staffing costs vary. For example the franchise is open on statutory holidays, which means she must pay her employees overtime. "My payroll goes from $4000 to $10000 for a two-week period. It is a lot of money, especially with the hours here. We are open eighteen hours a day." As if that is not enough, she must pay the franchiser monthly royalties of 11% "to keep the name" and cover advertising expenses.

Unfortunately Amy does not feel the franchise advertises enough. "I do a lot of my own advertising as well. You can't just go by what this franchise does." She has a huge file filled with advertising she has bought in the last year and a half. "I have done local radio…I do the coupon books…I've done a lot in the local bargain paper…I've done a lot in the community newspaper…flyers. I've done a lot through the local business association where I have put flyers into their handout."

Needless to say, all of these monthly expenses take their toll on this young business. While Amy still chooses to continue her entrepreneurial journey, she is considering the possibility of terminating it if her financial situation does not improve. She tells me later, "You have to know when to get off the boat. You have to know when to sell out. If you wait too long you have lost your chance. There are windows [of opportunity] to look at and you really do have to take advantage of those windows. And move on. I am hoping it will become, well, profitable, because I don't want to have to sell for a few years."

As Amy looks forward hoping for a future in the shop, she looks back with fond memories when she first bought the franchise. She surprises me when she begins her story. "I don't know why I have this store. This store was sold to another franchisee and I looked at another store…I sat in bed on night and I said, 'Who knows if there is a God above, but if I am to have this franchise, it has to be [this location] or nowhere.' At 3:00 the next afternoon, with no word of a lie, the phone rang. It was head office saying, "Amy, [that location] is yours. This is the first time in history that a franchisee has backed out of a store." To this day, Amy does not know why she got the very site she desired. However, she does know that she wants to keep this store. "I really do!"

Meanwhile the store is so quiet on this Saturday morning, one can understand Amy's concern. However, Jane lightens things up as she begins to fill Amy in about her latest plans for her upcoming wedding. Amy stops to listen with interest more as a co-worker than as a boss does. Then Amy teases Jane. The two laugh as Amy jokingly suggests that she will close the shop on Jane's wedding day so the staff can go to the church in their uniforms, even if they are not invited! Jane laughs as she quickly assures Amy that the whole staff is invited. Amy then laughingly suggests that they hold the reception in the coffee shop.

Amy returns to her bean counting behind the counter. One coffee-flavored bean is particularly low so she dashes downstairs to the coffee supply she keeps in storage. But before she leaves the floor, she calls to Jane to say where and what she is doing. Very soon she returns to the counter with three bags of the beans.

A few customers enter the shop for the next hour. When Amy knows the regular customers' coffee choice, she calls out the orders before they tell her what they want. The customers invariably smile when she does this and usually nod their heads in agreement.

One businessman asks Amy how business is doing. She answers honestly that it is slow but turns the conversation to him and asks, "How is your business doing?"

When she finishes making a latté for a customer, she catches the customer's eye and says, "Your regular latté, my dear!" in a clear, pleasant voice, making the customer feel special.

Throughout the morning, Amy makes sure the tables are cleared of all dishes and wiped clean as quickly as possible once the customer leaves. She places dishes in the dishwasher immediately if there is time, or places them on the counter beside the dishwasher if there is a line up.

As Amy cleans a table, she notices a customer's scarf has fallen on the floor. In one swift movement she retrieves the scarf and places it with the customer's coat on the chair beside the table she is cleaning. The customer responds with, "Amy, you're always looking after me!"

When customers ask, "How are you Amy?" her usual response is, "wonderful." Yet she is functioning on two hours of sleep and must be tired. Amy's general philosophy about customer service is that customers come in for a cup of coffee and light conversation. "When you are behind the counter and they walk in, they don't care how you are feeling. They don't care what kind of day you had. They don't care if your aunt died yesterday or your dog is sick. They will say, 'how are you?' And all they want to hear is 'fine'. And that is it."

Jane and Amy casually chat about a phone call Jane received at the shop by a former staff member the day before. He had just registered at a university out of town, and was calling to let them know how he was doing. Amy had missed the call because she was not in the shop at the time. "Did he give you his number?" she asks Jane. "No," answers Jane, "and he didn't want to call collect." "Oh," says Amy, disappointed. When a regular customer comes in, she and Amy continue to chat about the employee who had just moved away to start university. Conversation flows.

Between customers Amy and Jane continually chat as they continue to clear dishes off the tables, wipe the tables, straighten the chairs, place dishes in the dishwasher and set the clean dishes back on the shelves. An easy casualness exists in their relationship. "I am their friend. If one of my employees needs a bowl of soup, I will go and make it. I have taken staff different places. I have picked them up when they are stuck, when they have not had a ride, even at 2:00 in the morning."

As their friend and their employer, Amy never fails to be surprised by this group of young adults, her team. "Their ethics are phenomenal. I don't know whether it is just the core of kids I have or what…They are all from different backgrounds. Some of them come from bad homes with families out of work for years, sharing a two to three bedroom house with seven brothers and sisters. It has amazed me...Yet they are doing the job 100% of the time. Now and again we have a bad day. That is why we are a team. The other person picks up the slack. That is accepted. We are there for each other."

In turn, the staff treats Amy as a friend and one of the team members. For example, when she and her children moved over the Christmas season, the entire staff helped. "Some of them were at the beginning and they helped unload the first truck. A couple of them came on the second truck. A couple of them came when the trucks were unloaded at the end of the day. They said, 'What can we do?' Then they started unpacking boxes. One of them came and put my daughter's bed together. Five of them showed up at 11:30 at night for a glass of wine which they had brought...I didn't expect it. I didn't ask. They didn't offer it. They just did it!"

Today as part of the team on line, Amy makes a phone call from behind the counter. Being cognisant of a possible influx of customers, she does not take time away from the line to go downstairs to her office. She chats amiably on the phone much like she does with her customers, even jokingly asks for samples of something. She ends the conversation with, "You're wonderful. Thank you!" She then shares the gist of the telephone conversation with Jane.

Throughout the morning Amy nibbles on a cookie she has set on a plate at the back of the counter near the sink. She also keeps her cold cup of coffee nearby to sip over the course of the morning. Often an employee winds up throwing most of Amy's cold coffee down the sink so she can place the cup in the dishwasher. "The staff will tell you that I pour much of my profit down the sink. I really don't drink much coffee. In fact I drink much less coffee here than when I was at the clinic."

Amy rushes to serve customers. However, if they seem to hesitate because they do not know what they want, she steps back from the counter slightly and smiles at them. She does not hurry them but gives them a moment to think.

Amy continues to squeezes in her managerial tasks around serving the customers on line. She makes some notes behind the counter while watching for customers. She may be the boss but she takes her turn on the line very seriously. She drops pad and pencil to rush towards customers to serve them immediately, along with Jane. The two women act as a team, in a synchronised fashion.

A parent and two children enter the shop. While the youngsters want a muffin they do not know what flavours Amy carries. She leans over the counter and bends down towards the children. Then she patiently tells them the flavour of every muffin in the display case, as she points to each muffin. She talks directly to the children, encouraging them to talk directly to her. They in turn each choose a muffin. She hands each child his own muffin on a plate. Then with a great deal of patience she provides instructions. "You can carry this over to your table. Put one hand on the muffy and one on the plate" so the muffins would not roll off the plates while they walked to their places. Both children smile, and do as Amy instructed. Each of them manages to get to their table without a problem. After their mother pays for the order, Amy walks to their table to make sure the children get set up while their parent stands at the counter adding milk and sugar to her coffee. Later, the children return to the counter to look at the juices. Once again Amy bends down smiling. They indicate that they are still just looking. She merrily says, "let me know" and leaves them to look at the bottles. Soon they give her their order and happily jaunt back to their table, walking confidently with juice bottles in their hands.

Amy is in perpetual motion. For example, she notices a chair is slightly out of place, sets it properly at the table, and wipes off the table quickly too. She looks around to see what other tables and chairs need to be straightened. While walking throughout the shop, she chats with customers. "It is a joke on staff that when I walk through the shop's front door during the day, it can take fifteen minutes for me to make my way to the counter because the customers expect me to stop and chat to them."

Today she may stop to chat for two or three minutes to customers, but she quickly walks to the counter where she lines everything up neatly. She strides back behind the counter to refill coffee thermoses. This is obviously a very high-energy job. Amy is constantly on the move. Yet later in the day she tells me, "We were not very busy today."

When Amy places mugs of coffee on the counter for customers, she makes a point of turning the mugs around so they can grab the handles easily. For two senior citizens, she serves them a muffin and coffee, and asks pleasantly, "Now do either of you gentlemen need a hand?"

Customers chat to one another. Amy often brings customers into conversation with other customers when it is not busy. There is a friendly atmosphere created as a result. Music plays constantly in the background, not to interfere, but to add to the ambience of the shop. It is a friendly place to have a cup of coffee.

When a lady arrives pushing a stroller, Amy walks over, bends down to the toddler and playfully pulls on his cap, exclaiming, "Peek a boo!" Both mom and child break out in a big smile. Mom orders a cold drink. Amy makes sure she remembers a straw. Mom also orders a cookie for the baby. Amy places the cookie in a bag, walks around the counter, bends over, and hands the bag to the toddler, tips his hat and smiles at him. She then jaunts to the door to open it for the mother so she can easily exit the shop, pushing the stroller.

By 10:00 a.m. the constant flow of customers nearly fills the shop as many stay to enjoy their coffee and chat. As Amy pours a cup of coffee for one gentleman, she asks Jane to make a latté for his wife. Smiling, she then asks the couple if they want something to eat, or "have you had your breakfast already?"

The regular customers often place newspapers back on the rack or will offer it to other customers. There is a distinct family atmosphere in the shop.

The phone rings. Amy answers it on the first ring with a cheerful "Good morning, name of shop, Amy speaking." While on the phone she still turns towards the counter–waves at a customer and says, "How are you? That's good!"

Later when the elderly gentlemen clear the dishes off their table Amy laughingly says, "You can leave that to us for something to do!" They both smile and one replies, "I was feeling guilty." She asks, "Did you enjoy your coffee?" She does not know them as regular customers, but she purposely makes a connection with them when they carry their dishes to the counter.

By 10:30 sunshine replaces the rain. When a regular client dashes across the street from his own business Amy says with concern in her voice, "Hi there–no coat?"

Another customer chooses biscotti from a basket. Amy examines it closely, observes that is broken, and finds him a whole one. Another customer inquires whether they make sandwiches. "No, sorry," replies Amy. She suggests two shops that do make sandwiches.

One of the customers asks Amy if she will be in the next day. Often she is not on line on Sunday, but said she would be in for a coffee while her son was at sports. They discussed meeting at the shop to have a little visit.

A father and young son enters the shop. Jane serves them, but Amy takes time to smile at the child and say, "Isn't he adorable?" When the father allows his son to sit on a stool while he picks up his latté from the counter, Amy shows concern for the little guy by asking, "Is he ok there Dad?"

With a lull at 10:45 a.m. Amy seizes the opportunity to clean tables, and set furniture in place again, in between serving a few people. Jane continues to work the latte and cappuccino machines. It is not clear whether the two verbalised this to one another, or whether they simply have worked together long enough that it is automatic.

Amy empties the garbage as a customer comes in and says "Good morning Amy. How are you?" "Just great," Amy replies, while still doing the garbage. It seems many of the customers know her by name and chat to her whether she serves them or not.

At 11:00 a.m. Phil, the third staff member arrives. While Phil was not one of the original staff members, camaraderie exists between him and the two women. Amy remarks about his new jacket while he pours himself a coffee and they all chat behind the counter.

Amy mentions later that if her employees "don't work as a team then they leave." But she also lets her employees help choose new staff members. "Everybody works with the person on a shift and they sit down with me at the end of the shift. I ask, 'how did he/she make out? What did you find that was good? What did you find that was negative?'" She also puts the onus on the employees to help the person out. For example, they may tell Amy that the person 'hardly approached people.' She turns it around and asks them, "How did you deal with that?"

If some of the team members do not get along, she may answer, "Well, you know I haven't seen that but you have, so you work on it. You figure it out and I'm going to sit back on that shift and watch. I'll see if I notice what you have just told me about."

Amy encourages the staff members to take ownership of the situation. "They are the ones working hand in hand. I am not going to demean them for what they have noticed in somebody. It may be something really simple…I want them to work well…I leave it to them. I'll step in [only] if I have to."

Amy's approach to hiring staff and maintaining high standards for her employees seems to be working to her advantage. Her customers like her team. In fact, Amy believes that "the staff bring the customers back." One customer commented to Amy, "You have a lot of good looking people back here!" It turns out that some customers come in specifically when they know certain staff members will be on line. "They get to the point where they know everybody's schedule…one lady comes in all the time to speak to J."

Customers certainly come in to chat to the owner as well. When a gentleman enters the shop alone, Amy inquires about his wife. While Amy stands with a broom in hand ready to sweep the floor he chats to her about his wife who is visiting relatives in the northeast where they are experiencing a bad ice storm and resultant power blackout.

Three little girls stop to say goodbye to Amy before they leave. She turns and smiles at them. "Goodbye!" Meanwhile, another couple leaves and says "Goodbye Amy." She calls out, "Have a nice day!"

Yet another customer beckons, "Miss Amy, come here!" Amy laughingly responds with, "I'm just cleaning up after you—you made a mess." This customer had left one table to sit with a friend at another table. Amy adds, "Hold on darling while I put this [broom] away." She walks to the table and they share a funny horoscope with her. Amy turns, sees a line-up and races back to the counter, smiling.

These regular customers care about the coffee shop owner and her staff. These are the folks to whom Amy refers to when she says, "I think the people make the place." A few congregate at Amy's coffee shop both in the morning and in the afternoon for coffee and conversation. Their friendship includes Amy. "This group of people has gotten up and loaded my dishwasher, mopped the floor because I was on my own one day."

Amy makes a latté for a customer and asks her how much whipped cream she wants. The woman answers her and then asks if Amy is here all day. "Yes," she replies, "And it is about time." Amy had been with the accountant all afternoon the day before and feels guilty about not having taken her turn at the counter for long the day before.

Her experience with accounting in the medical field was so minimal in comparison to what she needs to know in the coffee shop business. "Although they call it *Simply Accounting*, I don't think any accounting is simple. It has been a real learner." Since it costs "anywhere from $35000 to $50000 a month to keep a coffee house running…you want to make very sure that the turnover is fast, that things are not sitting, that your labour cots are lower…so that has been a real learning experience."

When Amy first opened the shop labour costs alone were "95% of our take per month." She made numerous staffing changes. Five months after opening, about 24% of her take was labour and now staffing costs about 20% of her take. It helps that she was able to cut her staff requirements from 17 to 11 since she first opened.

One day she would like to take herself off the line, but for now Amy continues to serve customers. Clearly she enjoys the interaction with the people. Often she leans her elbows on the coffee thermoses while conversing with clientele. The topic can by anything from dogs to sports to current events. Yet when it is busy, she has a knack for keeping the conversation flowing while providing fast and efficient service.

When she punches the customer's card, if they hit the free one, Ann excitedly says, "You got a freebie–do you want to use it?" After every fifth coffee you buy at the shop, you get a free one.

At 11:10 a.m. the shop is three-quarters full with a line up. Amy takes orders while Phil makes the specialty coffees. When the orders are taken and paid for Amy helps make the special orders to speed up the service. While making these coffees, she talks sports scores to a customer sitting across from her. When another customer comes in holding a little dog, Amy exclaims "how cute" and chats to the gentleman about dogs.

The background music stops. Amy encourages Jane to choose the next selection. Amy only sits down to drink coffee when a businessman arrives to show her artwork. She looks at it with a critical eye and tells him directly what she likes and does not like. She continues to watch the line while discussing the artwork. She rushes to the counter to help serve. There is a constant flow of customers so the shop is almost full.

Many clients like the atmosphere. They come every day to chat together and drink coffee at Amy's shop. In fact some who have become regular customers in the shop have befriended one another in Amy's establishment simply because they have seen each other daily in the same place.

Amy is called to the phone. It is brief call. When finished with the phone call, she turns around to greet yet another regular customer. He buys a pound of coffee and leaves the shop. Many customers are not rushing out, however. They often sit at least a half-hour chatting casually in what seems to be a favourite place on a Saturday morning. They greet one another when they enter the shop and call out goodbye to the owner when they leave. As people sit at one table they frequently greet others at another table, creating a very convivial atmosphere.

Six teens from a swimming club enter the shop. Once served they check in the back corner to see if the "comfy chairs" are occupied. They congregate in this little alcove where they sit on old, comfortable stuffed chairs looking out one of the two back windows. The tiny white lights strung on willow branches beside one of the windows adds an enchanting dimension to this cosy area.

By noon the shop is almost full. Customers continue to ask, "How are you Amy?" and she still answers, "Wonderful, how are you?" It is busy and she must be tired because she has only sat down for very short spurts of about five minutes at the most. Yet when the four women leave (those who read her horoscope), Amy is not too busy to call out "Bye ladies" to which they respond with "Bye Amy." They all sound like old friends.

The teens leave, but not before clearing off their table, placing dishes on the counter and pushing in their chairs. They too call out their good-byes to Amy.

She notices Phil has made hot chocolate. There is no line up, so she asks Phil to bring the hot chocolate to the older gentleman who had ordered it and then had sat a table to wait for it.

By 12:15 there is no line-up. Amy makes more coffee in the huge thermoses. When a young boy comes to counter, she asks, "How are you?" and adds, "Do you need anything darling?" He shows her a special pen he has and she takes time to play with it. He orders a donut. He then drops his money on the floor. Amy asks, "Can you find it?" He can and hands it to her. She puts change in his hand and closes his hand over it so he does not drop the change. She continues to play with the pen, and then ruffles his hair while saying, "I like that!" He walks to his table with a big smile.

At 12:45 Amy runs downstairs to prepare a deposit in her office. She has a monitor in the office so she can keep an eye on the shop when she is at office. Amy had a 24-hour security camera installed when she initially opened the shop. "We don't have security here…[we are not] in a mall where guards are going by." In addition, having the camera and monitor set up allows her to watch for long lines at the counter, so she can dash upstairs to help serve.

She picks up the telephone on the first ring, answering with a professional voice. She tells me that it is her mom is calling. Since Amy has already talked to both her son and daughter, she says, "Now it's mom's turn." It is a quick call to organise today's activities with her family after work. Her parents live nearby and often spend time with Amy and the children. She depends on them to help out with the children since the beginning of her entrepreneurial journey. For example, her parents often pick the kids up after school or a baseball game, or stay with them when they are ill. "Home suffers. You have a choice."

She openly discusses maintaining a balance between her personal and professional life as an impediment to the entrepreneur. "The hardest thing for me has been balance–between home and business. And I think a lot of women find that…It doesn't matter whether you are a mom at home or a mom at work, when mom goes home, they expect mom to have everything in order…From what I see in my friends too, it is mom who is supposed to be there. End of story. I mean you can work, you can have a career. But you are supposed to be home, dinner, and whatever. The most difficult obstacle has been balance."

Amy believes that the entrepreneur must decide "what price you want to pay and if it is worth it." While convinced there are both positive and negatives about owning and running her shop she still worries about the effect her entrepreneurial journey will have on her own children. "You don't know the damage you are doing and you don't know the good your are doing. And I am sure there is both."

As a child, Amy grew up with an entrepreneurial father who was a self-made millionaire. His wife quit nursing to have her children and then helped in the family business. However, the family patriarch did not allow his daughters "to work in his business because it wasn't for young ladies to do." Ironically all three of his daughters own their own businesses now.

But they grew up in a very affluent home with little knowledge of how hard their father had to work. "My father kept it separate. We never knew the financial problems of the business or what he was going through. We have a very good idea now going through it ourselves."

As the parent/entrepreneur, Amy does not keep home and business separate. Her daughter works on the line with her. Her son wants to work on the line, but is not old enough yet. So her children know what is going on in her business, just as her staff knows most of what happens in her personal life. Indeed, Amy admits that her personal and professional lives pretty well "mesh together".

While still in her simple downstairs office that houses a desk, a security monitor, and two chairs, Amy calls in the milk order. She is pleasant, and does not sound rushed. She tells them, "We're very slow today." There is some problem with getting the exact order due to a computer breakdown. Amy replies, "No problem. Just go with the order from last week. You can't help it."

Before rushing off to the bank to deposit the money, she runs upstairs to help serve again. Once the line up is over, she puts on her coat to quickly walk to the bank so Jane and Phil will have time for their lunch before she leaves at 3:00 p.m.

When Amy enters the bank she greets all the tellers, mostly by name. They in turn are greet her with, "Hi Amy! How are you?" She asked one of them, "How are your children?" She listens to the detailed answer. The teller says there is one mistake in the deposit and when she is about to show it to Amy, she responds trustingly, "That's ok. Just change it." Then she quickly asks for change for bigger bills. She adds it up quicker in her head than the teller can! In fact she says to the teller, "You have one extra roll of dimes there for me."

Amy lives in this community and, as a shopkeeper, takes an active role in the various community events. It is obvious that she interacts with many of her neighbours as she walks back to the shop greeting a number of people along the way. Sometimes they greet her first with a big wave, a smile and "Hi Amy."

Although being part of the community as a shopkeeper translates into costing the business money, Amy enjoys participating. "I couldn't keep track of all the functions I have joined…I think that is part of being in the community…I think you have to…I don't think you can not be part of the community when you are in the community."

By 1:45 p.m. she has returned to the shop and is pleased to see a former staff member who dropped in to chat about his course in animation. A customer joins the conversation and Amy tells him that he is a wonderful artist. She continues a lengthy conversation about his future and about his former co-workers while tidying the tables with him following her around. It is analogous to the way family members catch one another up on the news.

When watching Amy with staff members it is obvious that she measures success in terms of her relationship with them. In fact when asked if she puts her staff ahead of her customers her answer is a resounding "Yes. I think I have to. I can't say it enough. This is a hell of a job. I had no idea—it is physical, it is a mental kind of thing…I think staffing is very difficult…And I also rely on my staff…My staff is a real asset."

Perhaps the best example she can cite that clearly demonstrates that she sets her staff relationship above that of her customers is when she had to decide whether to remain open on Christmas day. The franchise fines its operators if they close that day. However, Amy asked her staff, "Does anyone want to work Christmas?" When they responded negatively, she closed the shop. Yet she knew that some of her clientele would have congregated in her shop that day. "It is kind of sad…because I know a lot of people in my immediate area were customers who are regulars who didn't have anywhere to go."

Today there has been a lull but by 2:00 p.m. the tables are full with two people waiting in line. Fifteen minutes later it is quiet again. Another employee arrives early to have coffee with his girlfriend before starting his shift. He chats to Amy and the others behind the counter for awhile. Chuckling, Amy finally tells him, "Go have coffee with your girlfriend!"

It is 2:30 p.m. when two customers return. They had already stopped for coffee earlier in the morning. They inform Amy that they had just had lunch and are now ready for more coffee. Amy jokingly asks, "Where's my lunch?" They reply, "It blew away!" Lots of bantering seems to go on between Amy and her regular clients.

While Amy puts her staff ahead of customers, she certainly has demonstrated her interest in the customer throughout this Saturday. In return, many customers have bonded over the past year or so with Amy and her staff. "[It] is fun when some of the customers come in and share their lives literally…I didn't expect that…It is neat…the baby's first year birthday we had here. The mom actually went into labour here. She came in for her cappuccino even though she was in labour. I said, 'this really isn't a good thing to have when you are in labour.' I was timing contractions and then off she went to the hospital. The baby is almost 15 months old now."

When describing various customer stories, it is as though they are family members to Amy, much as her staff seems to be. "It is a really big family in here, and it is growing with the customers that come in. I can't keep up to it. It amazed me."

At 2:40 p.m. Amy fills the coffee urns again, cleans off tables, replaces chairs. She stops to serve customers. Then she continues to clean. This time she wipes down the glass display windows. She interrupts her cleaning to chat to a couple with their dog, bending down to say hello to the dog and pat him. Then it is time to sweep the floor again. This time she asks Phil to do it since there is not a line up.

At 2:50 p.m. Amy stands at the end of the counter, quietly surveying the shop. She jots down some notes. Earlier she had indicated to me that since she had not been on top of things during her move, she noticed that staff had not done routine things. But then she also added that it was her fault because she had not been leaving instructions at the end of her shift. Today she was writing notes for the staff.

At 2:55 p.m. there is another line up. The tables are full again. Amy takes time to chat to customers she knows yet continues to pour coffee and work the cash register.

Although it is now 3:00 p.m. and the end of her shift, Amy continues to serve until the line up is depleted. She finally fixes herself a bagel and coffee, and sits down alone at a table to eat lunch while watching her staff working. She makes mental notes so she can ensure the place runs smoothly without her. Her day is officially over, but during her lunchtime she watches her staff and decides how to manage them better. She will soon leave the shop to go home for family activities. It is a struggle to pull herself away from her own enterprise to go home and play the role of mom. It is a balancing act in which she has such high expectations in both her personal and business life, that Amy finds it difficult to admit, "I can't even meet."

Yet she stays. She continues to work long hours as her own boss. She continues her journey into entrepreneurship with others. "[It is] the combination of staff and customers." When she takes a moment to reflect on the business, she acknowledges "I think the people make the place." What makes the entrepreneurial journey worthwhile for the coffee shop owner? "[It is] the combination of staff and customers!"

CHAPTER TWO

▼

KNOWING THE "BOTTOM LINE" TO KEEP CONTROL: BARBARA, RETAIL FABRIC STORE OWNER

When Barbara first opened her own retail fabric shop, working for herself was the prime reason for becoming an entrepreneur. Part of the enjoyment of controlling her own destiny is knowing she can calculate the "bottom line" daily. Barbara refers to herself as a financial manager who looks at the numbers all of the time. Right from the onset of her entrepreneurial journey, this businesswoman considered knowing the "bottom line" an important aspect of running her own operation.

Barbara's father owned his own accounting firm, and her grandmother was a clothing designer. Although she seemed to always know in her heart that she would follow in their footsteps as an entrepreneur, it was not until Barbara saw the age of 35 looming ahead that she felt she simply had to begin her own journey. "I was completely driven–nothing was going to stop me. I'm glad I did it! Is it some midlife crises or something?"

Now over three years into her journey, Barbara is considering the possibility of terminating it. "Your priorities shift. I think the possibility of working for somebody else is there." Working 65 hours a week while earning $2000 monthly is taking its toll. She knows she could be earning $100,000 annually working for others. However, she is only in the exploration stage of selling her business. With a twinkle in her eye, this creative retailer discusses an alternative enterprise. "I think the direction I am going now is towards more commercial work if I can get it. So finding ways to pursue that is the trickiest part, whether going on the Internet or just going door to door, whatever."

Prior to opening her own enterprise, Barbara managed a fashion retail business for thirteen years. Her annual salary of $25,000 to $30,000 working for a retailer in the women's shop fell far below that of the male managers' $50,000+ working for the same retailer in its men's stores. The retailer refused to give her a raise so they came to an agreement. "They gave me six months severance package and I said thanks a lot and left."

Eventually she embarked on her own entrepreneurial journey, and with that came numerous changes. Overnight Barbara became owner/operator of her own shop, but had little money or time to share with her husband…"Our lifestyle really shut down when I started my business because we pretty much put all of our money into it. We're not going out for dinners anymore, going shopping or going on holidays the way we used to when I had a good income and he did. We had a real nice lifestyle." Since then she has been working at finding a balance between her life as an entrepreneur and her personal life to create a lifestyle that works for her. "I think it is so important to really balance your life."

At 9:33 on a cold Tuesday morning in January Barbara pulls up in her van, parks it outside of her home decorating retail fabric store, and jumps out. She walks smartly to the front door of the store, opens it, and with a quick hand movement turns the lights on, barely pausing to even feel for the light switch.

Glancing around the store Barbara takes in her environment in one sweep. Everything is perfectly in place. At the front of her shop the tall racks of fabric rolls hang neatly. She strides past the cutting table that is tidy and completely cleared. Her eyes do a quick search of the organised swatches of fabric samples hung neatly around the perimeter in the back of the store. Her inventory of fabric is a large part of the business. "Managing inventory is a very tough thing for anybody." Barbara found that after about two years it becomes a little more obvious what sells. Fortunately, the trends can last quite long in the home decorating business. "It is not like fashion that only lasts a season." People spend a lot of money on home fashions. "They want it in their homes for at least five years or so, so because of that the trends stay around for a while. Your inventory doesn't get obsolete as quickly."

When she walks past the sales counter near the back of her shop, she automatically reaches out to flick on the computer. Barbara swiftly opens the door behind the counter, hangs her coat on a rack in the little staff room/kitchenette and reaches for the vacuum cleaner.

It is only 9:37 a.m. when she swishes the vacuum over the sales floor picking up stray pieces of thread. Barbara has not slowed her pace since jumping out of her van. "I move all over the floor, never stop seemingly."

Perhaps it is Barbara's height that gives her a particular presence. Her straight brunette hair falls gently to her shoulders, which softens her businesslike manner. She wears olive green wool pant/skirt, tall brown boots, wheat-colored cardigan and turtleneck with a patterned scarf at her neck. One can tell at a glance that she once worked in the fashion business with her flare for putting herself together.

By 9:45, having completed the vacuuming, Barbara puts the vacuum cleaner in the back room. She strides to the wooden table placed in the back of the room in the centre of the fabric samples. Two plaster-of-paris sconces sit on the table. She picks each sconce up and examines it closely. She painted them yesterday, but does not like the finish now that they have dried. "They are awful. I used pearl paint and I don't like them at all." She whips out two more sconces from a shelf where she stores them. She hires a craftsperson to make the sconces for her shop and paints them for her regular customers. She applies a matte finish on these two sconces.

At 9:55 a.m. the telephone rings. The caller is one of her best sewers. Initially they discuss business but the conversation soon turns to the problem Barbara has been having with the landlord. "I will not get hosed by anyone because I have lawyers in the family, so I know what to watch out for!"

She explains the incident more fully to me later. "Re-negotiating my lease this year was just ugly. It went on for months." The landlord demanded a huge rent increase that would have put her out of business. "If they got the increase they wanted then my business was instantly not viable. I had to point out to them very forcefully that a bird in the hand is worth two in the bush!"

Prior to these negotiations Barbara had actually hoped for a slight decrease in her rent since she considered herself a good tenant throughout the last three years. "We'd always had a fairly god relationship up until then and I just had to chuck that all out the door. They thought I was being unreasonable, but from my perspective I wasn't being unreasonable. Either we came to the agreement I wanted, or I was out of business. So it was really, really important. I didn't care what they thought of me."

She hesitates a little when she thinks about relationships. After all, she is a friendly woman whose existence depends on her ability to provide good customer service in her own business. "You do want to have good relationships with people and you want people to like you. It is human nature." However, she has been on her entrepreneurial journey for three years, and has worked with people throughout her varied career. "You have to have a pretty thick skin. In terms of customers I certainly do. People can be nasty. If they have had a bad day or they are not happy with whatever, they can take it out on the store person…You get tough after a few years."

Another experience that helped her 'get tough' involved dealing with banks. In her second year of operation she had been given a $10,000 line of credit by one of the financial institutions. When "it was at about

$9999" Barbara's banker was due to be audited; they told her she had two weeks to bring her line of credit to $0. She nearly exploded over the telephone. "You have got to be kidding. You thought it was OK for me to carry this loan. I had for months and months. All of a sudden I'm not worthy just because your auditors are coming?" She had doubled her sales and her cash flow was twice as good as it had been. However, no amount of discussion, screaming, or cajoling on Barbara's part changed the banker's mind. "It was absolutely absurd. Completely absurd."

She and her husband devised a plan. "Our mortgage was coming due and the banks all want your mortgage." They approached another banker. "If we give you a line of credit for my business and his [her husband's business] then you get our mortgage. They said ok. They gave us what we needed which was great." So Barbara paid off her $10,000 line of credit with the first bank within the two weeks. It lost her business, her husband's business, and their personal business. "So it was really short sighted [on the bank's part]."

Cash flow continues to be a headache for this independent shopkeeper. "As you grow you have more money going out and bigger bills to pay. And the money just never seems to be enough. I am always just a little behind schedule on payments and things." When she doesn't pay her suppliers they will sometimes refuse to send new shipments. A bad month can put her behind in payments, although she never owes any supplier more than $20,000. "And doing ten times that in sales–it should not be a problem, but it seems to be. It is a big outflow. So that is really stressful."

When a supplier refuses to send a new shipment of fabric it means she needs to stall the customer, or become a creative problem solver. For example, a customer ordered fabric from a sample book whose supplier refused to ship more orders until Barbara made a payment. "I found exactly the same fabric from another supplier and got it for the customer and did not have to pay the first supplier. Pretty creative!"

In the shop today Barbara's organised, methodical side seems to control her every move. She uses her time wisely and efficiently. Since she was already interrupted by the telephone call, she proceeds to make a few calls of her own. One is on behalf of her husband who runs his own construction company while another is a call about her payroll.

At 10:10 a.m. Barbara's first customer walks in with a sample in hand and strolls around the shop looking at a variety of fabrics. Still on a business call, Barbara informs the person on the other end of the line that she must serve a customer, ending with "OK darling".

Barbara walks over to help the customer choose fabric. She shows a simple curtain treatment to the customer who says, "I'm just learning how to sew. I thought of making just a valance."

They discuss trim for a simple finish on a valance, but the customer does not look convinced, and asks Barbara, "Can I just show you something. I have a pattern. I just got the [sewing] machine for Christmas."

Barbara examines the picture on the pattern and tells the customer how to sew the curtains without a pattern. "I'm sorry, but these patterns…" The customer cuts her off with, "For someone who doesn't know how to sew though, the pattern is a good idea." Barbara had understood that there were only instructions in the pattern envelope. "Oh, so there is a pattern in the package?" The customer answers, "Yes, there is tissue." Barbara uses a calculator to add up the metres of fabric required for the curtain pattern.

Barbara then walks towards the counter where she has a rack of sewing books for sale. She provides the woman with a few additional ideas in a helpful, but business like manner. First she indicates a book of curtain styles to the customer. "They have photos for every step. It is my favourite book." She then points to another book with cushions and accessories in it. "These are excellent books too." Finally, she suggests a large book full of a variety of sewing projects. "A Singer book."

At 10:25 a.m. another customer walks in the shop, briefly looks around the front of the store, and leaves within a couple of minutes. Barbara looks up, aware that the woman is in the front of her shop and watches her while allowing the first customer a minute or so to peek through the suggested books. Once the second customer leaves, Barbara turns back to the first woman to point out another book that designers use saying, "Just sketches–for ideas." As an example of what she means, Barbara opens the book to a particular page of valances. "Here's a whole bunch of different scalloped valances."

The woman looks keenly at the book, noting "I could not draw that on newspaper." Barbara patiently describes how to do it. "Fold the paper in half. You just have to cut one side and the other will then be exactly the same."

The customer is delighted and interested. She asks Barbara, "Are sheers hard?" Barbara answers immediately, and honestly. "Sheers are tough to sew because of the synthetic fabric."

While the customer begins to browse by herself Barbara puts the rolls of fabric that they were looking at back in place. But she watches the customer while tidying up and walks over to the customer to confirm that the fabric she is looking at is suitable. This peaks the woman's interest and she asks about trimming the fabric. Once again Barbara can tell her exactly how to do it. "Use your zipper foot and stitch close to the edge." When the customer admits she has no knowledge about the zipper foot Barbara patiently tells her how to use this attachment.

The client asks Barbara's opinion of a specific trim for the suggested fabric. "Yes, that would be nice."

The woman feels comfortable laying out the pattern on the large cutting table located near the front of the shop, asking more sewing questions about the waste of money if she buys patterns for placemats and other accessories. Barbara confirms that it is a waste and tells her how to trace patterns from placemats she already owns. They continue to chat about sewing. Barbara laughingly acknowledges "my friend taught me not to be afraid to rip out anything."

In a courteous and helpful manner, Barbara helps the customer choose a curtain rod, along with the fabric and trim. As Barbara rings up the sale, the woman remembers she needs materials for two windows and apologises for the inconvenience. Barbara laughs and makes sure she gets fabric from the same dye lot before cutting it. They discuss the size of the needle required to sew the fabric. Barbara knows the answer and willingly indicates the size she should use.

The customer discloses that she has many windows in her new house. Barbara demonstrates an awareness of the woman's financial concerns when she suggests the client start with cheap blinds and eventually buy fabric for more expensive window coverings, adding that she knows that is never cheap in a house with so many windows.

Since Barbara has advertised her business in many ways, she asks the woman what marketing tool drew her into the shop. "How did you know about the store?" When she first opened the shop, for example, Barbara distributed brochures. "That is really costly…and I really didn't get a lot of response from them." She has been advertising in the local town paper, as well as writing home decorating articles for publication in the same paper. Currently she is contemplating placing advertisements with a large metropolitan daily newspaper to generate more business. "We can draw from quite a broad area. I think I would get more out of my advertising dollar than just placing ads in the local paper. If I could do both, I would. But I can't so I might try that for a few months this spring to see what will happen."

Meanwhile the customer today had not read any ads or brochures about the shop. "I drove around and saw the place!" she exclaimed to the shop owner. That surprised Barbara since her shop is located in a small strip plaza, rather than in a mall or on the street where customers would frequently stroll by such a shop. "Good luck! Here's my card. You can call." says Barbara. The lady laughs and asks, "If I get hysterical can I call?" "Yes I take hysterical sewing calls!" says Barbara laughing.

Barbara carries the rods to the cutting table where the customer's pattern is still lying, and then places the fabric back on its roll. Meanwhile the woman continues to talk to her while putting the pattern back in the package. Barbara tells her about sewing courses available through a local college.

When the customer thanks her for all of her help, Barbara smiles, "Oh you're welcome. Goodbye!"

It is now time for her mid-morning tea. Barbara swiftly glances at the cutting table making sure all is in order again. Another customer walks in, looks around briefly and leaves. Barbara quickly strides to the backroom to put the kettle on for tea, keeping her eye on the shop.

Before the kettle is finished boiling, an older gentleman comes into the shop. He asks for a specific size of string. Barbara apologises for not having that particular size, but shows him the available sizes. The customer leaves without buying a substitute size.

Another elderly gentleman returns samples he had borrowed the day before. Barbara notes that his wife has not accompanied him this time. She asks if they chose a fabric, which he confirmed. However, he indicates that he wants his wife to be with him when they order the fabric. Barbara tells him she will not be back in the store until Thursday. He appreciates the information and indicates they will come in then to order the fabric. Barbara had spent so much time with this couple that she knew they would normally want to order through her, rather than one of her employees since they would have to start all over again indicating what they wanted.

The next door neighbour enters through the door between the two stores holding a large picnic table umbrella. Barbara laughs at the sight of a summer umbrella in the middle of winter. They seem to have a good relationship as tenants in the same building. They open the door between the two stores to help keep her shop warmer. In the winter he sells fireplaces and always has some turned on, which generates additional heat. It takes a lot of gas to heat the fabric shop with its high warehouse like ceilings, so Barbara appreciates the neighbour's help.

At 11:00 Barbara finally sits down at the back table to drink tea. Between sips she works on the sconces again. She examines the matte finish. She does not like it any more than the pearlized finish.

At this moment the landlord walks in looking for the rent cheque. Barbara explains that she had stopped by the landlord's restaurant the night before to drop off the cheque, but the lady had not been there. Now she does not have the cheque at the store because she inadvertently left it at home. The landlord leaves.

The telephone rings. She carries on a brief business conversation. Her manner is business like, yet friendly.

The telephone rings again. A customer inquires about the status of her order. Without having to find the information, Barbara quickly and efficiently responds with the exact date the order will be delivered to the shop.

About noon another customer arrives. As Barbara walks towards her she asks the woman in a very personable manner, "Did your hubby like it?" The customer confirms that he did, and states the yardage she requires. Barbara reaches for the roll of fabric, and begins measuring it out on the cutting table. She glances at the woman's expression, and catches a look of apprehension. "It looks like a lot when it is all spread out like this!" The customer plans to sew curtains. She seems to have a much better idea of what she is doing in comparison to the woman earlier in the morning. Barbara does not provide a lot of little tips, but fully answers the few questions the lady presents to her. They discuss the rods the customer requires. Barbara wonders whether the customer wants them today or once she finishes the project. "You don't want them hanging out the window on such a cold day!" Once again, she looks at the situation from the customer's viewpoint and verbalises what may be worrying her. She then suggests that the client could cut the rods to the exact size, giving explicit directions without the customer having to ask.

Next Barbara cuts drapery lining. Although the client does not ask about the fabric, Barbara informs her that this fabric is water repellent to protect the curtain from humidity. Barbara enjoys passing on her knowledgeable about her products to the client.

Barbara finishes cutting both fabrics and rolls each one on cardboard roll, which she carries to the back counter where the computer is located. At this point the telephone rings. She answers it in a business-like fashion, but once she recognises the caller, her voice becomes very friendly. "Oh hi

J." While on the phone, she rings up the sale for the customer. She ends
the phone conversation with, "Thanks a lot J., bye." She then quickly and
ably puts a plastic bag over the fabric on the roll. She looks at the bill and
tells the customer, "The printer did not do a good job." She rings up the
sale again without appearing to be flustered. As she rings it up again the
customer realised that she had forgotten something. She will have to pay
separately. They both laughed at the same time. Barbara picks up the rolls
of fabric and carries them to the customer's car. It is a cold winter's day,
but this is part of customer service. Once back in the store, she immediately puts fabric rolls away and tidies the cutting table.

Barbara glances around to ensure that all is back in place. She now takes
the time to make a telephone call to a friend. There is no answer, so she
leaves a message on the answering machine. Even when leaving a personal
message she does so in an efficient, business-like manner, carefully listing
a number of things she wants to chat about. "That's it, see you!"

Next she makes a business call. "Hi B., got a minute to talk?" She waits
for his response, and adds, "You called me." She discusses selling her business, including her stock. He had shown some prior interest and she wants
to consider the possibility. Barbara knows what she wants from him. She is
very straightforward and not the least intimidated by him. She indicates
that otherwise she may have a big sale and liquidate. "I'm not interested in
talking about it unless you want the whole deal…otherwise no use discussing it…Thanks. Goodbye."

It has been just over three years since she opened her shop.
Nostalgically, she relates the story to me of her most memorable moment
at the outset of her entrepreneurial journey. "It was when they put the sign
up in front of the store. That was my business name I had registered! I got
the sign made and they put it up. The truck was up there installing it. I
went and stood back by the road to look at it. I got all choked up. I was so
proud! My own business. It was for real. You know it didn't seem real until
that point. That was really exciting. That sounds so goofy." By the time

she finishes the story she was laughing at the picture of herself feeling so proud and excited.

The pride and excitement were the culmination of her dream of running her own business from as far back as she remembers. "I had always thought about it while working for other people and decided at the end of my last job that the time was right." She had not exactly planned when she would start her journey, but once she had received severance pay and saw 35 years of age looming, she knew she had to begin that journey.

While she had family background in the entrepreneurial field and had taken some university courses on the subject, she prepared for the role of entrepreneur. "I went through a course that the government sponsored—a self-employment assistance program. They set up an eight-week course at the time. They went through, step by step, how to create a business plan. At the end of the course if your business plan is accepted then they give you additional support and incentives."

With her business background, Barbara had little problem creating a business plan and having it accepted. Once she had decided to open her shop, she received an offer. "I had a really good job offer, like six figures that I turned down…It would have been almost $100,000 a year and I said no. That is how badly I wanted [my own shop]. He said, "You are out of your mind!" But she set off on her entrepreneurial journey.

While the business is currently not floundering, it is not paying back high enough dividends at this juncture of the journey. She remembers the kinds of things she and her husband had once enjoyed before investing most of their life savings into her entrepreneurial venture. "We had had a real nice lifestyle. We were willing to forfeit that for a certain amount of time. But time is up now and he has kind of had enough of being poor…I agree with him." It seems she may decide to give up owning this shop to have more money. However, "if I have a really fantastic spring then it gives me freedom to do other things." Those other things may include commercial work.

She describes one of her most unforgettable commercial jobs when she had been in business just over a year. Her husband had built a day care centre for a corporate client as part of their building. He got the designer's name and address for Barbara because he realized that they would require window coverings, pillows, and seating for the 15000 square foot area. When he suggested that Barbara call them and offer her services, she said, "oh you have got to be kidding! That is way over my head. It is too big!"

However, after a little more prodding and encouragement from her husband, she called and spoke directly to the designer, who appreciated Barbara's initiative. Nobody else had called them and this international company had only sourced out locally at that point.

When asked to send them samples, Barbara had none to send. "So I solicited a couple of sewers and a workroom and we made up a bunch of samples–5 or 6 pillows, seating, and other appropriate items, and sent them to her."

A little over a month later Barbara had the contract for the entire building! "They gave me the whole job. I was terrified because it was so big." She ended up making about $70000 from that one job. "I was horrified the whole time because it was so big and I was so new in the business but as I went along I had things planned in my head and it really went off without a hitch. It was a huge success for me and I was really happy about it and really happy that my husband pushed me to do it." Barbara knows from experience that she could conduct business more on a commercial level and earn good money, so that is definitely an option she may try rather than selling her store.

But for now, Barbara's priority is running next door to buy a sandwich for lunch. She switches on the answering machine. When she returns three minutes later she sits down to enjoy her lunch. She often reads during her lunch hour. In slow months like January she may read up to ten books a month at work.

This owner/manager spends a lot of time alone in the shop because when she has staff in the shop she obviously has to pay them whether there are customers are not. "And I am free!" She usually has her staff work in the shop when she takes her day off. She currently enjoys a good working relationship with her two part-time employees, but it has not always been that way for this sole owner.

Her first employee was a good friend with no retail experience but with sewing and decorating expertise. "All the rules that they tell you not to do, I did. I should have known better because I had been in retail for so long. But I thought, 'I want to enjoy my atmosphere and have somebody I really like to work with.' But when it came to bringing in the dough, I was doing 90% of the sales. She was doing 10%. I was actually paying her probably a lot more than I was paying myself because I paid her monthly. I wouldn't take money unless there was extra money sitting in the bank, which there never ever is. So that was a big mistake."

It was difficult to tell her friend that she was not selling enough to make her salary worthwhile, but Barbara was getting frustrated. "If it had gone on any longer it would have been the end of our friendship." Barbara had to fire her friend. "I was very upset about it. I was ten times more upset than she was! She said 'OK I'll go back to my life, take care of my kids, see you later.' But I was saying "Oh my God, it's the end of an era.""

Barbara then hired a woman with many years of retail experience, but this proved disastrous too. First of all, the computer system completely confounded her. "I would be telling her things 3, 4, 5, 6 times–the same thing and it wasn't sinking in. I couldn't figure out why." Secondly, she did not have a handle on the fabric. "She wasn't suggesting things to customers or she would say 'we don't have that' and we did!"

Barbara hired another part time employee who had worked for her before. She was a very good, professional sales person. Being older, she had little interest in putting in full days at Barbara's shop. She and Barbara set up a pact. Once Barbara found good help, she would resign because, as she said, "I'm just going to golf full time now."

It was not too long before Barbara finally found good help. One of her suppliers had a daughter who was working in retail, but wanted another job. Barbara hired this young, energetic woman. "She has just been great."

Barbara's second part time person is an interior designer who was one of Barbara's customers. "She knows how to sell because she is in people's homes." This woman brings in customers since she is still a decorator who works about seven hours a week in Barbara's shop. "So that is great. She is out there hustling...So she has been really good for business too."

After three years Barbara feels she has finally resolved her employee dilemma with herself as the full-time person and two part-time women who can take charge while she is out of the store. "So they are in place, and I think that is all the staff I need for now."

Meanwhile, having only two part-time employees means Barbara spends most of her working days alone, except for her customers. Perhaps this is the reason she has found that she likes having decided to close her shop on Sunday. Now she can enjoy the company of friends and family on Saturday nights and Sundays.

The reason she originally closed on Sundays was to create a more balanced lifestyle. "It is important to really balance your life and work can become everything. When you are an entrepreneur you obviously have workaholic tendencies that can take over because you enjoy it so. You are most comfortable when you are doing it. You know when you are at your work that is where you feel most comfortable."

Although she has been enjoying her entrepreneurial journey, Barbara confesses that the stress of being the boss goes hand in hand with the freedom of being the boss. However, she disciplines herself to take steps to offset the stress. "You have to keep yourself personally, mentally, and physically fit...when you are in business." She can put away the concerns of the business for a few hours by "being with friends and family and just talking about other things, other interests. That is what really distracts me about worrying about the business." She also works out. "I go to a gym right across the street here so it is right in my face when I leave the store. I work out at least three times a week, two hours a session. It is very, very important to my mental health."

A fringe benefit of her networking plan turns out to be a stress releaser. She plays baseball in a league, as well as joining other sports. She signed up for the baseball league very purposefully. "They are on my mailing list and everybody sort of flogs that baseball list because they are exactly my target market…they have been very supportive. We all support each other." Just how supportive is this group of players? "I do have a lot of customers coming in from sports organizations that I am in…I would say if I went through my ball league list I would say that I am up to about 60% of the people in my league having actually bought [merchandise] from my store."

Unfortunately none of her baseball league friends support her today. It is one and one half hours before another customer arrives. The client thought Barbara was busy. "No I am all yours," Barbara responds laughing. She laughs a lot with customers. She genuinely enjoys them. Yet prior to opening her own business she had taken some personality tests to ascertain what she would be best suited to do as a career. "One of the personality tests said this person in no way should ever work with the public!" She laughs now, but then she was devastated. "I thought oh my gosh I should be hiding in a back room sewing somewhere!" Fortunately, she "took that with a grain of salt because I do like working with the public."

The customer indicates that she is looking for crushed velvet fabric for a priest's chair that sits in the church sanctuary. Barbara points out a few samples, but she realises that the customer is having problems making a decision. The client suggests bringing a couple of books filled with samples to the priest to allow him to choose his own fabric. Barbara agrees and proceeds to write the book numbers and the customer's name in a notebook before handing the sample books to the woman.

At 2:30 yet another older woman, well dressed and perfectly groomed, comes in asking for various ideas for window covering. So far the clientele have all been middle aged or older. Barbara points to one of the many displays of curtains she has hung around the shop, much as one would see in a showroom. Most of them are placed above the fabric as a way of filling up the wall space since the warehouse ceiling is so high. Barbara has these made up from her fabric by the seamstresses she hires. "It is a big expense when you make up fabric in a drape or a piece of furniture. But it is hard to picture the fabric made up for most people, so this really helps."

On the coffee table in the sitting area at the front of the store Barbara has placed home decorating magazines filled with ideas for different drapery styles. She uses post-it notes to identify certain pages. Then she can flip through the magazine quickly to illustrate a certain style to a potential customer. "I show them something because they can't picture it made up so I just go to my little post-its and say, 'this is what that looks like made up.'"

In addition, she has created a photo album with pictures of window treatments made with her fabrics. "Most are commercial projects that I did and some are pictures that customers have brought me that I asked them to bring in." Her album has proved to be successful. "That is a really good thing to show people too." She continually updates the album.

She and her customer look at the venetian blinds in her shop. They discuss the customer's tab curtains that do not pull across the rod very well. Barbara provides a solution. "Dust builds up there. That's why they don't slide very well. This sounds like a crazy idea, but just spray the rod with PAM or something like that so the tabs can slide over them. Tabs look great, but they are not very functional." She also suggests having curtains with the metal clips, not tabs, because they slide much better over the rod. They then discuss a seamstress for the curtains. Barbara has a number of sewers whom she uses on occasion, usually for commercial customers. However, she willingly gives their names to customers who wish to contact the seamstresses themselves.

The client discusses fabric designs for her curtains. As she provides Barbara with more specific information the shopkeeper helps her find a variety of possibilities throughout the store. They discuss delivery time for custom fabrics, as well as cheaper solutions. Finally they return to the discussion of her tab curtains. It is now 2:45 p.m., and the customer says,

"Alright thank you for your advice." She mentions having to measure correctly. She leaves the shop. Barbara knows that this is normal customer behaviour on their first visit. She recognises the shopping trends of her clients. "It is a research visit. They look, ask a lot of questions, take samples, and then leave."

Meanwhile another customer has walked into the store while Barbara was discussing the tab curtains with the last customer. When this client indicates that she is browsing Barbara leaves her alone.

Three minutes later a young customer comes in who had visited earlier. Barbara recognises her and takes her directly to the rack of fabrics they must have discussed before.

The phone rings. She answers on the portable phone that sits on the cutting table at the front of the shop. She politely asks the caller if she can call back because she is with a customer. She quickly returns to the client in the shop. They discuss the amount of fabric required, based on the size of her bay window. Barbara demonstrates her knowledge when she says "Huge bay!" Furthermore, she provides hints on how to both cut and hem this particular material as she cuts the fabric. She slides the roll into a bag and rings up the sale quickly and efficiently. The young woman asks one more question. Barbara answers it and then laughs. "Little tricks!" The customer leaves and Barbara immediately walks over to the cutting table to clear away the fabric.

The cold, gray afternoon continues. By 3:05 p.m. there are no customers in the shop, so Barbara takes the opportunity to catch up on her bookkeeping. As a former business major she has no problem knowing how to get to the bottom line. "I have a business degree so you do a lot of number crunching in four years in business school." She is amazed that in the self-employment assistance program, out of fifteen people in the 8-week class, she was "virtually the only one who had an accounting background because you really need that stuff. All those people wanting to start businesses—that is really scary to me. You have to be able to measure your success." She crunches numbers a lot and knows exactly what is in the bank–or not! She is now working on year-end and month end. Her accounts are computerised. "This software is great."

In doing her month end for November she realizes that she overpaid a former employee for that month. At 3:45 she immediately telephones the woman and explains the situation briefly. The employee admits that she thought it was a larger sum than normal. Barbara knows to the penny how much overpayment she is due. "Just make out a cheque to the store." There is no problem because this is the former employee who is also a friend.

She continues working quietly on her books for another ten minutes until an older couple walks in. She looks up from her computer and immediately walks toward them. They think they want tapestry fabric, but when she shows it to them they decide that it is too dark. They mention a fabric by name. "Oh that's different." She shows them that fabric, but it is exactly like the lady's friends and she indicates that she wants something different. They tell her it is for dining room chairs. She shows them other durable samples and then leaves them to browse.

Barbara carries an array of sample books providing a huge selection of styles. "Pretty well anything goes today." For the sales person this means, "you have to peg the customer and go from there. You have to figure out what your customer wants." People want the choice to decorate in their own style. "People won't be dictated to anymore."

However, Barbara indicates that there are trends in the industry. To keep up with the trends she attends seminars, particularly focussing on major interior design seminars. "They are really comprehensive. They have world class designers come in and give you colour forecasts." She also reads trade magazines and home fashion publications.

Meanwhile, Barbara clears the table in the back so the older couple can spread their various samples out on it. The husband indicates samples that he likes but his wife does not see anything particularly that she likes. Barbara stands by to help them, putting samples away as they refute them. She makes other suggestions. She listens to what they say and then responds with samples of colours and designs she thinks they may like.

She says very little as they look through the samples, just quietly flips through books for them. She suggests that they bring some home to browse with at their leisure; however they leave without any samples.

At 4:40 p.m. Lynn, one of her two part-time employees, comes in to visit. They chat amiably. She is the interior designer who was Barbara's customer. Lynn now works in the shop about seven hours a week. They chat excitedly about the gourmet gadget sale she is hosting at her house the following night.

Five minutes later a customer comes in, and Barbara immediately walks to the front of the store to serve her. After discussing samples Barbara shows her, she leaves.

While Barbara serves this customer the telephone rings, Lynn answers it and willingly responds to answers the caller's queries.

Lynn and Barbara chat a little more before Lynn leaves. It is now 5:30 p.m. Barbara does not expect that anymore customers will be in for the day. She goes next door to chat briefly with her neighbours, before leaving the shop early.

While Barbara enjoys the freedom of owning her shop and being able to close a little early on a cold winter's night, the question remains whether she will continue or terminate her entrepreneurial journey. "I have got the store for sale. I might not sell it. Or I might do this. Or I might do that. I like having lots of options. I do like the uncertainty." She and her husband discuss these options at length. She acknowledges that "I can only do something full tilt for 3 ½ years. I don't even do the five-year thing." It is the idea of creating something new that excites her. "We'll either wind it down, or sell it, or carry it on." For this entrepreneur discussing a detour in the journey seems to start the adrenaline rushing through her veins again. "I was really interested again."

CHAPTER THREE

▼

BALANCING HER OWN CUBICLE: DIANE, FREELANCE WRITER

Diane contracts her writing skills to commercial firms and also writes articles for various magazines. She has run her one-person operation for twelve years, with the last five on a full-time basis. This self-assured writer does not really consider herself an entrepreneur because she is a one-person operation with no inventory to worry about. Diane balances her day between working in her upstairs bedroom of her family home producing various writing projects, and being a mother who attends her children's games and school events.

Diane seems somewhat non-committal to the idea of being a bona fide entrepreneur. "I mean I am in some ways, but I really think when someone takes a huge risk by buying a product or opening a store…having an inventory, [then she is a true entrepreneur]". In fact when asked exactly when she opened her business, she really did not have a date. With a sense of humility she says, "As a writer, when do you open? You have a computer. You have a pen. You have business cards."

Her demeanor changes quickly to one of enthusiasm, however, as she relates the story of her decision to work in a field that she loves. In her early twenties, Diane found work as a technical analyst with a company but only stayed for three months. "It was a terrible job." She landed a similar position with an insurance company. Once again she was not enamoured with this job. "It didn't really occur to me to change fields. It was more I didn't think about changing jobs." Then her mother died. "It sounds so corny, but it really made me think you only live once. It took me thirty years to figure out this is it! And if you don't do what makes you happy in that time well then you sort of missed the boat."

Diane decided that she wanted to work for herself. She broke the news to her husband over dinner one night not long after her mother's death. "I think I sort of want to quit my job and be a writer." She quickly adds that her husband thought she was a little crazy. "However, he knew that if I made up my mind he was powerless to say anything."

Diane's resolve to write on a freelance basis surprised her entire family because she does not come from a background of entrepreneurs. Her mother was employed off and on as a sales clerk for a variety of companies. Diane's father "worked for the same company for thirty odd years. He worked there for the rest of his life, until he retired…The world has changed. In those days you could work for someone for thirty years and have a reasonable income and security."

Sitting in her small home office now she laughingly tells me the reason she continues as an entrepreneur, "Well there's mortgage, there are children…" But she rushes to add the real reason she continues to operate a one-woman operation. "It's not just the dollar. I do get a lot of satisfaction out of doing the work. I do enjoy it!"

It is 9:25 on a cold Monday morning in January. When I ring the doorbell to Diane's home her husband, Paul, opens the front door and greets me warmly. He indicates that Diane is upstairs in her home office and must be on the phone since she did not come down to greet me herself.

This is a surprise because she had thought this would be a slow morning and was not planning to begin work until 9:30. Diane enjoys the flexibility of working from her own office. She has an answering service so she can be flexible with her hours. "If I want to go on my child's field trip, or whatever, I can."

However, flexibility can also lead to wasting entire days if she is not goal oriented. She admits that she makes jokes with other writers. "When you don't want to write you do the laundry, or bake cookies, or something." However, Diane is pragmatic about her entrepreneurial endeavour. "If you don't put enough time in you're not going to make enough money." She understands that she must be disciplined; and recognizes the advantage of creating objectives for herself. "When I want to do something on a beautiful summers' day...I want to go for a walk so I have goals: as soon as I finish this I'll go for a bike ride."

Today she sits at her desk in her small office, waving for me to come in as she continues a telephone conversation. She is discussing a terrible ice storm in the Eastern Ontario /Quebec area of Canada over the weekend. Her biggest client has numerous branch offices in the area. She is on the line with one of the branch managers. Diane initially demonstrates concern over their power and heat shortage. "What are other people doing–staying with people they know?" She then expresses concern about their businesses. "Hope your power stays on–when I hear it may take weeks–every day I now thank a higher power that I have power." She eventually says good-bye and hangs up.

In a quiet, unassuming way Diane then greets me with a quick "hello". She explains that she must continue making telephone calls. She gets on with the business at hand. Both her physical appearance and clothing mirror her quietly, efficient manner. A slim woman of medium height, Diane holds herself very erectly even when chatting on the telephone or working at the computer. Her black hair is neatly cut short in an easily managed style. She wears just a touch of makeup. Her long jean skirt, black leotards, and suede mules, however, indicate a casual side to this otherwise efficient businesswoman. The bright fuschia turtleneck under a long navy cardigan sweater also provides a hint of a woman with a sense of humour within this capable entrepreneur. Later, when discussing her attire, she indicates that she does not have to be dressed in a business suit for the two afternoon meetings she will be attending, and certainly not for when she is sitting in her home office.

Diane continues calling her client's various branch offices throughout Eastern Ontario and Quebec to ascertain whether they are open for business due to the shut down from the storm over the weekend. She leaves a message at one office. Then she talks to someone in another office, ending the conversation with "Good luck to you!"

She immediately checks her own telephone messages. A message from Patrick, one of the managers, provides her with a report on their situation. She leaves a message in response to his.

With a little information from a few branch offices Diane begins writing a bulletin describing the situation as it pertains to her client. As she thinks about what to say, she types rapidly. After two short paragraphs, she remembers to save the bulletin as a file. She returns to rapidly typing the text.

Patrick returns her call, indicating his anxiety about the storm situation. Diane responds with concern for another manager saying, "When I talked to her, she was almost crying as she described how communities were helping each other and the client's offices were helping." Patrick evidently asks Diane whether she has started writing a special bulletin that will be issued company wide across Canada that day. "Yes, I've started writing it already...I'll keep writing what I have and I'll keep adding to it as I hear from people...Alrighty, bye" This was a quick call. She returns to the keyboard. She edits as she inputs the bulletin; changing words, adding capitals.

Someone knocks rather loudly at the front door. Diane leaves it up to her husband Paul to answer the door. Two minutes later Paul brings a package to her office that had been delivered by the courier.

The telephone rings again. Diane answers it in a businesslike tone. She immediately begins taking hand-written notes in a steno pad she keeps by the phone. "I don't think we realised until Friday how serious the situation is". She then pushes the steno pad away from her and chats briefly about the ice storm with the caller. "I am waiting to get calls back about how things are fairing..." She then gets to her point; she asks for the information for another bulletin she is working on for the same client. As they discuss this other information, Diane pulls out a file from her desk drawer beside her. She makes changes to this bulletin's hard copy about an employee award. She had already written and sent a copy to this manager. Now she would make more changes. "I will fax a draft to you...guess I should do it today...we don't know where you will be tomorrow...OK, I'll do it right now then."

When she completes this phone call, she turns to me saying, "I have to remember to do other work besides the bulletin about the storm." With that said, Diane finds the file referring to the award in her computer files. She cannot ask one of her employees to work on something for her because she has never hired anyone to work for her. "I sub-contract to people, but I don't have employees." Diane explains her reason for having no employees now or in the future. "I can't imagine that because I would have to move into an office ant that's a whole other thing. And I don't see that happening." She clarifies that in the past she has sub-contracted writing assignments. "If I have a big writing job, I will give a piece of it to somebody else."

Running a one-person operation could easily lead an entrepreneur into the trap of never taking time off. But Diane has learned that she can take holidays if she prepares in advance. "I would tell my regular clients ahead of time. I would send them a fax or an e-mail about my being away for a week or three days or something." As for someone who happened to call when she is away, Diane has little concern. "For the occasional people who use me twice a year, well, if they call me and I'm not here, then they would just have to wait." She also provides alternative solutions for her occasional clients. "One time when I was going away for a week or ten days I made arrangements with another writer and she uses me in the same way.

If you have an urgent communication need call so and so. She does the same thing when she goes away so at least you don't feel when you go away that you are leaving people high and dry."

Diane exudes confidence and control as she discusses operating her entrepreneurial venture. She ensures that her regular clients know and understand that she is on her own. This means that they need to realise that she may not be available whenever they need her. They still retain her services. Diane does not allow herself to be too concerned about not being in the office due to some unforeseen problem such as accident or illness. "I don't think you can live your life worried about 'what if'". Diane reflects back to a time when her family was young to clarify her stand on not worrying about things. "When my kids were babies I never gave them bottles and I never kept breast milk in the freezer. People would say, 'what if something happened? What if you were sick?' I can be a worrier, but in all the years my kids were growing up, never did the situation ever, ever come up where I couldn't take them with me or I couldn't feed them. You know, here I would have been sticking all these bags of milk in the freezer and probably throwing them away and worrying about it!"

This competent woman also indicates little concern about the actual operation of her entrepreneurial business. For example, over the years she has disciplined herself to maintain precise billing records. Before starting work on the next project of the day, she pulls out a desk shelf and marks down her hours on a time sheet that she uses to clock in minutes spent on each project for each client. She can then charge specific departments within the same company for the various writing projects she does for each one. She calculates her time in fifteen-minute segments if she is going from one task to the other, as she finds herself doing this particular morning.

Once she has marked her time spent on the storm bulletin, she calls another client to inform her that she is working on the awards bulletin and will fax the draft to her shortly so the client can be at the fax machine to receive it. Diane explains that "it is an award that nobody knows who the winner is so she has to take it out of the fax machine quickly." She completes the draft with a quick spell check. "My spelling is bad today." When the suggestion is made that it is because she is being observed and interviewed, she replies very honestly, "No, usually if someone is looking over my shoulder I do, but you're not looking over my shoulder. It's just me! I'm going too fast." It is a stressful day for her as she prepares this storm bulletin. She then admits that she has an herbal tea that she drinks sometime to calm her down.

Diane must then call another person to explain the changes to the impending awards bulletin. She makes it brief and to the point, ending with "ok, bye." While she carries on this telephone conversation Diane saves the changes to the file. She wastes little time. She prints the news release. She reads the hard copy of the release. She edits the hard copy before making the same changes on the computer. At 10:15 a.m. Diane methodically marks her fifteen-minute interval again on the time sheet.

Diane runs downstairs to have her husband proofread the hard copy of the award bulletin. She quickly returns to her office just as the telephone rings. "Hi Sally. "No, not yet dear. I'm getting there...I don't want to have 40 people in my kitchen...I have to get off the phone because I'm waiting for a call. Talk to you later, bye." Sally is a fellow writer/friend who understands that Diane is in the middle of something and cannot chat today, although Diane's tone is both pleasant and friendly.

Her husband runs upstairs with the proofread copy. He circled the few corrections required. She briefly informs him she will have another release for him to proofread later, namely the storm bulletin, once she has received all of the information regarding the store damage from the various locations. When later asked what she does when her husband is not there to proofread her material, she had a quick answer. "I have others I can send it to for proofing. It would be difficult if you were totally isolated."

She tells Paul that she plans to send a release to a newspaper soon. She reminds him that, from her experience and perspective, Americans usually know little about Canadian news but if it is important enough, they run it.

She returns to her desk to make yet another call to her client telling her the award bulletin is ready for faxing. Diane ensures that the client is ready to receive it. As she double-checks the fax number before sending it, she remarks, "I'd be in real trouble if it were not the right number." She certainly respects the confidentiality of her work.

She then calls her other client to inform him that she is e-mailing the storm bulletin so all the employees across Canada get an update on the situation in Eastern Ontario and Quebec. If she receives more changes, she promises to call him to discuss whether another e-mail should be sent. Diane makes few moves without receiving full client approval.

Diane focuses her attention on another article for the same client's upcoming newsletter. She telephones Bill and leaves a message of precisely what she is doing and what she needs to finish her article. The message is concise, articulate, and yet friendly. To ensure a quick return phone call, she leaves her phone number.

At 10:50 a.m. Diane takes time to open the package delivered by the courier. She immediately begins reading the material enclosed. The telephone interrupts her reading at 10:57 a.m. She answers in a business-like tone giving her first and last names. "Hi Bill. How are you doing?" They discuss e-mailing the storm bulletin to the client's employees across Canada. "If we do send something out—who should we send it to for approval?" Diane took notes in her steno pad while listening carefully. She then repeated the names back to him.

At 11:04 she makes another call "Hi there! Getting tired of these phone calls?" Once again she discusses her last telephone conversation. "Did you get my e-mail by the way?" They discuss further changes to the draft. "Alright. Have fun!"

While Diane has not had a minute all morning to herself, she seems to be having fun working on the various projects and making numerous phone calls. Having been in business for twelve years, Diane finds most of her days are filled with paid work. However, on the few slack days she fills in the gap with unpaid work, just as she did when she first started her business. She well remembers those days! "I would read things. I would read about writing. I would read about the business of writing. Or I would go to the library to do research…There is always something to do. There is always marketing. There is always research. When you write for magazines you are always doing research too. Yes there were times when probably I was here and I wasn't doing any paid work, but I was working." That was how she managed her business at the beginning of her entrepreneurial journey when business was slack.

Throughout the morning Diane displays her current and very practical management strategy. For example, at 11:12 Diane makes a change to her personal schedule that she has on computer. "I add things and I have to put things on to tomorrow sometimes." Diane has set up two schedules, one for the week and another for the month, so she can see both at a glance.

Once she completes entries on her personal schedule she pulls out her drawer to jot down her client time again for future billing. "If you don't keep track of your time then you can't bill your time…It just becomes a habit. I don't even think about it…ok I am switching from this newsletter to this report so I just open up my top desk drawer and write it down." Diane acts as her own bookkeeper. "I keep sheets and I tally up my hours and I invoice. I try to do it in batches, but I don't want too much time to go by because then you don't get paid." She makes it sound so simple, although she does confess to hiring an accountant. "I only use him for my taxes and occasionally for a question. I do all my own bookkeeping. I have a program on my computer that I keep track of things."

Tracking her own billing seems to present little problem for this entrepreneur. She uses a spreadsheet to work out her tax credits. She laughs about having to do it separately and not on her computer program. "My software version is older and it does not accommodate that very well." This is one businesswoman who spends relatively little time on her books. "It takes about an hour maybe an hour and a half every quarter."

Today Diane does not waste a minute. Once she marks down her billing time, she reads more from the courier package until 11:20 when she begins to prepare her briefcase for her afternoon meetings. As she inserts a couple of file folders, she mentions that she has been waiting for information from this client since September to complete a magazine article. The magazine wants to do a longer article than she had originally sent them, but the client is slow in getting the additional information to her so she can expand on it. The client runs a very small operation.

At 11:25 she tells me "I just have to go downstairs for a minute. That is when the phone will ring." She switches it to answering service and runs downstairs to talk to her husband for a minute. The telephone rings, and the answering service picks up. When she returns to the office, Diane immediately plays the message back. Another branch manager tells her the draft copy is not accurate. She returns his call, introducing herself as the regular writer of the client's monthly newsletter and other articles such as this bulletin about the storm and the resultant shutdowns. "We just ran with the information I had at the time." She makes notes on her steno pad while listening to him. "That would be perfect. That is just what we need…OK that's important because we want to be accurate." She asks for information to be faxed to her so she can edit the storm bulletin again. "Thanks a lot, Gord, and good luck to you!"

At 11:38 Diane listens to the message that came in while she was speaking with Gord on the other line. She returns the call. "Hi Nancy! I was surprised you're there. Are you just picking up messages or are you there? I understand the office is closed today. Will you be open tomorrow?" She listens to the information. She responds in a business-like way, but uses a caring tone. Then she sits back in her chair and chats about the storm situation. She tosses her pen down and quietly listens before saying goodbye. She indicates later over lunch that this woman seemed to need to talk about her personal experiences with the storm, and Diane felt compelled to listen.

Diane handwrites notes on a stenographer's pad when she is on the telephone. She transcribes these notes on the computer as soon as she completes the telephone conversation.

She makes good use of the time as she is waiting for the latest fax from Gord, to enjoy a little time with her family. Her husband has prepared a pizza lunch and we sit at their dining room table chatting about the ice storm and the various comments she has heard all morning from her client's many branch office managers.

Fifteen minutes later she is back in the office. Gord has faxed the information to another office by mistake, rather than to Diane. She must wait for this office to fax the information to her. Time is running out quickly since she must leave soon for her appointment with another client. Diane is concerned the fax will not arrive quickly enough for her to incorporate it in the storm bulletin before having to leave. She debates whether she can re-schedule her afternoon client meeting. She calls this woman only to find that she is not currently in the office.

Finally the fax arrives with Gord's information. There are few changes to be made. She immediately re-types the storm bulletin making the necessary changes. Even though she is in a hurry, she spell-checks.

She begins to look in her briefcase for something. "It was a Christmas present and I am still not sure where I want to store things!" There are lots of zippered compartments. She likes organization. Her office is very efficient, very organised just like she.

She prints out the latest draft about the storm and runs it downstairs for her husband to proofread. Once re-read, the latest bulletin is sent electronically to the client's office. Diane also calls to tell the client that she has made the appropriate changes and has sent it by e-mail.

Although she is in a hurry, this efficient businesswoman reaches into her drawer for a new file folder and handwrites a label. She places her hand-written notes from her notepad in the file, along with the hard copy of the bulletin. She puts the file in her active file drawer in her desk. She hand writes labels because it is a waste of time to print out computerised labels. She has filing cabinets in her basement filled with old files that are labelled by computer. "But who has time now?" she laughs. This full time writer has more important things to do with the hours in her day.

After working full time for the last five years, Diane seems to indicate that she does not work hard at marketing her writing business. When asked about obstacles in her business, she considers for a moment and suggests "trying to gain business I guess. Again just doing your networking, doing your marketing, writing a newsletter that I send out to clients and prospects." But then she later confessed that "sometimes I feel like I'm not moving forward. I'm sort of in the status quo. Sometimes I move forward by getting new clients and by getting new jobs from existing clients. Sometimes you can be proactive in marketing, and at other times it just falls in your lap, so I'm not always working to move things forward. Sometimes they just move regardless of what I do."

When encouraged to provide ways she has moved her business forward, Diane demonstrates her creativity and resourcefulness. For example she created her own website. "The website is sort of one part of the way that you market yourself, but it is just a small part." For Diane networking has proven itself as a good way to get known. "I go to these networking meetings, or the Chamber of Commerce...You go there. You show your face. Everyone gets a chance to introduce him or herself. You give a 30-second little commercial. So you do that. So when people think writer, they think of you...Really it is the networking more than anything else."

Since Diane writes for a living, she creates her own newsletter promoting her entrepreneurial endeavour. "I have my newsletter. I mail it out. I bring it with me. I bring so many copies to these [networking] dinners."

Diane realises the necessity of having to promote her own entrepreneurial endeavour, yet does not express anxiety about obtaining work. She almost seems to enjoy the ambiguity of not knowing what is around the corner. "There is the element of the chase. Now when the phone rings, with call display you basically know who is calling, but at the same time it can be a surprise. Every once in a while you get a call from a new client, or from an old client you haven't heard from, or whatever, or an existing client calls with an interesting project. You never know. Tomorrow I could get some wonderful things happen, or nothing. So that is kind of exciting."

Part of the excitement for this writer is the money she can make as an independent freelance writer. She laughs as she tells the story about what her brother said when she first went into business for herself. "I told my brother and he didn't quite know what to make of it. He said, 'So let me get this straight. It's like doing homework and you get paid for this?' I said 'Yes'. So now he still asks, 'Are you still doing your homework and getting paid?' And he says, 'I should have paid more attention at school. I could be sitting at home like you instead of working.'"

Diane quickly adds that satisfying her clients excites her, makes her feel successful. She had surveyed her regular clients a few months prior to this interview. She does not hesitate to share the results of her little survey. "All were very satisfied with the work I had done. That made me feel good. So I thought well at least I must be on the right track if I'm not losing clients. You do lose clients sometimes for various reasons, but for the most part people were happy with what I was doing."

On an even more personal note, Diane discussed what her business meant to her. She adamantly believes that the entrepreneurial experience does not only have a monetary value attached to it. "It's not just the dollar." For this writer, being challenged is part of the success of running the business. "You like to feel that you are learning something…And you like to do new things. It was more than six months ago that I was asked to project manage someone's website. That was good because that was using some skills I had but I had not been paid to use before. So that was good. I guess you always have to look at where you are and see sort of where you want to go."

It is now 1:05 p.m. Diane has driven 15 minutes to meet with a leather refurbishing company owner. They greet one another in a business like fashion. As soon as Diane sits down in the cramped office, she pulls her file out and begins. "Betty we wanted to expand on the leather article." Diane both initiates and controls the meeting. She has her notepad and pen in hand, ready to write down the information immediately. She introduces me. "I left a message to say Darlene would accompany me." The woman nods her head. The business meeting is in full swing.

The owner tells Diane that she has a mascot for the company: a cow. Diane laughs at some of the cartoons the client shows her depicting a cow in a variety of ways.

The owner then tries to download her marketing plan from the computer to provide Diane with the necessary information for the magazine article, but it is taking too long. Diane sits patiently while the client attempts to now stop downloading. Diane reminds her that this article is in its first draft. The owner provides Diane with some written material as background information for the article.

Diane asks specific questions to encourage the owner to think of additional materials. While Diane does not describe herself as creative in terms of a short story writer, she demonstrates creativity when she formulates the questions for the owner so she can expand this article on leather refurbishing.

This freelance writer often finds herself having to be creative. For example, for most magazine articles it is usually the writer who originates the topic. "You have to come up with the idea first and present it to the editor and they say yes or no. Sometimes you present these ideas and six months later they say 'we want that article on such and such. That's a really good idea for an article'…Even with corporate clients, sometimes you have to drive the process."

As a writer, Diane finds that she sometimes knows her topics. For example she writes articles for a parent's magazine. "For those magazines I learned from having kids." She laughs at this because these were certainly hands-on research topics. For other ideas, she researches. "Like just before I was about to go into the parenting news groups on the Internet. What are people talking about? What are the issues? I get ideas there."

After answering a few of Diane's questions the owner of the leather refurbishing company runs out of time and must leave for another appointment. Her husband/partner joins Diane in the office. Diane quickly and efficiently fills him in on the information she has received from his wife, while reading her notes. Diane refers to a fax received from the magazine that describes what they want in the article. As he provides the information she continues to take notes. Frequently she stops him and summarises the information she has written down to ensure it is correct.

She also patiently waits for him to make a call to the West Coast to procure authorisation for a reference name that he wishes to include in the article. A few times Diane glances at her watch but then sits back in the chair to relax a little while he gets the information. He rings off and she reads from her notes to remind him where they were. He continues to supply information verbally to her. She now has enough for the article. She tries to bring the meeting to a close with, "I'll have something to you in a few days." However, he wants to discuss the use of the cartoons in the article. She makes alternate suggestions to his which he seems to approve. They say goodbye and Diane is out of the office by 1:55 p.m.

Diane discloses that this is a small client that will not use her services often. She can easily complete the first draft of the article in a few days. When asked how she handles a much larger writing assignment, Diane shows no sign of being nonplussed. She recognises it as a little bit of an obstacle. However, she has an answer. "Something that is really difficult to write or something that is hard to research or maybe working with a difficult person...I guess you just take one at a time. I find usually the way to work around those things is to break them into smaller parts. For example, with a writing project you can break it into really small parts then it doesn't become a big challenge."

Fifteen minutes later we arrive at the executive meeting of a local writers' association of which she is a member. We are ten minutes late for the meeting, but she had told them to expect her to be tardy since she had a back to back meeting with a client. The group greets both of us warmly. Diane had told them beforehand that I would be accompanying her.

Everyone chats and laughs together. There is a good rapport, and great camaraderie among these writing peers. Diane is past president so she is not in charge of the agenda, but acts in more of an advisory capacity. Members of this group and others like it keep Diane from feeling isolated as an independent entrepreneur, she tells me later. "Sometimes I meet one or two people for lunch. Sometimes it is picking up the phone to call someone…then you bounce something off them."

Diane explains later that this network of writers communicates with one another, thus preventing the feeling of abject isolation. "When I get a really juicy assignment that usually makes me feel good, I come downstairs and say [to my husband] 'Guess who just called? Guess what I am going to do?" He just looks at me and says 'so?' Then I call up another writer, and they get exited. Or a writer friend will call me and she'll say 'I'm doing an article for a major monthly magazine!' And I say, 'Oh wow great!' She'll say 'You know I told my next door neighbor and she didn't understand why I was so excited.' And I say, 'that is exciting!'"

As this executive meeting of writers begins the business of the day, Diane pulls out her notepad and pen. Throughout the meeting she makes notes of the things she volunteers to do.

They discuss future full meetings. She listens and adds a few astute comments. She seems very knowledgeable about venues, topics, and interests of writers in general.

Diane confirms a time for a future meeting and adds, "I'll put in on the website." They have a website for this group and it was Diane who set it up and continues to maintain its changes.

When one of the members of the executive does not really want to call a printer, Diane volunteers to do so. She had had contact with the printer a few years ago and does not mind making a call.

Diane indicates the number of people who have checked their website. Of her own initiative Diane suggests that she put something in the writers' newsletter about the number of people who have checked in the website to keep the association informed about the use of the website.

They discuss future meetings. Diane suggests holding one in May. She then offers her home as the venue. She ascertains available dates in May for the event in a very accommodating way. With that the meeting is over at 3:20 p.m. In the car, she turns to me with a smile and says, "Now you know why I attend these meetings. They make me laugh!"

Twenty minutes later she is back home. She greets her children now home from school and her husband who had met them at the bus stop. She stops to ask each of the children "How was your day?" She listens attentively for their answer.

By 3:50 p.m. she is back in her home office upstairs. She checks messages on her telephone, fax, and e-mail. For Diane greeting the family during her workday has become the normal pattern. She admits that her business and her home are "really closely intertwined. Especially if you are working at home. If you are working in another office, even if you are self-employed, you can compartmentalise more. But I am here! I mean if I am getting dressed in the morning and the office phone rings, maybe I'll pick it up. It depends on what time it is and where I am going…So it would be different if I were working somewhere else. I think that is the point…the fact that I am working in my home, I think the person and the business person is the same."

Diane had to learn how to be a businessperson working in her home. She talks about achieving a balance between the two so she can cope successfully with being an entrepreneur in her own home. "It has become easier now that the kids are old enough to understand that when I am on the phone in [my office], come back in a few minutes unless it is an emergency." She recalls when she had one youngster and was pregnant with the second that a client wanted her to do more work than she was interested in doing at the time. "I just didn't want to do it. It was towards the end of the pregnancy, my energy was down." However, she has learned not to tell clients her personal tales of woe. "You can say it'll get done, I'm working on it tonight, or whatever, and you just do it."

On occasion she has allowed work to infringe on her family life and she did not appreciate it. She tells one story. "There were a couple of times I missed [kids'] soccer games because of clients. It only happened twice and I swore I would never do it again because it made me really mad. The client wasn't organised and I missed this game. That's because they did everything at the last minute. We need you now. Edit the copy now. It's about 6:00 p.m. Two hours. So something like that just bothered me." She now knows how to handle such clients. "I wouldn't even answer the phone." She laughs. This is one woman who knows how to balance the family and the business with a sense of humour.

She is one of the fortunate entrepreneurs whose spouse also stays home now. He didn't always work from home; he used to commute into the city daily. Diane could not set up early morning appointments because she had to get the children ready and off to the school bus. "Now I can have a meeting at 8:00 a.m. Not that I like to. But if a client needs me." Furthermore, after school Diane had the same dilemma when her children arrived home from school and her spouse was working in the city. She found alternatives when necessary. For example, she began exchanging favours with other mothers. "I would have another person pick up the kids at the bus stop—one of the other moms who stays at home. You know, say is it ok if the kids go home with you. People at the bus stop are great. You talk to them every day. You do the same for them. You pick up their child or whatever another day. So it is fine. I didn't have to do it that many times. So it wasn't so bad."

Diane really appreciates having her husband home now so she can attend conferences, or schedule a few business trips. "I think when you don't have a partner who is around, it is more difficult. Then the balance becomes trickier. But now I can be here talking to you and I know dinner is getting started. I make the salad tonight."

At the same time, Diane was quick to confide that while she is a family person who attends her kids' soccer games, she does not forget her entre-preneurial side. "I think when you are a writer, you and your business are very close because you are always thinking...When you go to a soccer game with your kids and you are meeting new parents, in the back of your mind is 'I wonder where he works. I wonder where she works.' Does she have a need for a communications person?'" She divulged that the family plans on visiting Florida in the spring break. "I was thinking maybe I could do a travel article. Then I thought, 'Do I want to be working when

I'm down there?' And I thought, 'Sure maybe I could do a travel article and pay for part of the trip.'"

At 3:59 p.m. she calls a client back about one of the projects and makes the changes to her news release immediately. At 4:05 p.m. she marks down the time spent on this client. She keeps track of all work on one time sheet, rather than on individual sheets for each client. The second method makes it too easy to miss billing a client. For Diane it works better with one sheet that incorporates all jobs. This way she can then check it off once she has billed a specific client.

She telephones another client about updating the upcoming newsletter with the latest ice storm situation. She makes suggestions for timing and reminds the client that they need time for the French translation. It is a short call.

Now that she has been at two meetings this afternoon it is time to input the dates and items to do in her calendar on the computer. She then files her hand-written notes.

By 4:30 p.m. this entrepreneur is ready to finish reading the notes she received in the couriered package today. She tells me it will take her 20 minutes and she will call it a day.

Upon departure I take one more look around her small upstairs office that she shares with her husband who now runs his own small business. Two computers, two office chairs, and two bookcases almost fill the space completely. The cream walls and gray furnishings create a sophisticated, efficient, business-like atmosphere. However, Diane's framed degrees and certificates hang beside treasured family photographs and children's drawings over her desk. The physical juxtaposition of her personal and professional life serves as an illustration of the balance this businesswoman maintains between home and work. I remember her laughing when she glanced around at her office. "I wouldn't see why I would leave. Leaving would mean working for someone else, which my clients have offered me a few times in the past year. But I feel like saying 'Why? I have my own cubicle. Why would I want to be in your cubicle?' I am not interested."

CHAPTER FOUR

▼

CONTROLLING HER OWN DESTINY: SANDI, LASER TECHNICIAN/SALES REPRESENTATIVE

Sandi contracts part of her time as a sales representative for a collagen company and the other part of her time as a laser technician/collagen treatment specialist for a cosmetic surgeon. She officially works out of a corner of her basement, but spends most of her time away from her home office. Her entrepreneurial journey has followed a spiritual route that led her from deep depression through a watershed of fear to a passion for controlling her own destiny and creating a balance in her life.

As she describes her life six and a half or seven years ago, Sandi finds it almost incredulous that she could have come so far on her entrepreneurial journey. "Being an entrepreneur was nothing that I had ever dreamed of doing!" She had been married to a man who was out of work since 1984. She was a full time nurse who took a risk "after twenty years of institutionalisation where I had a pay cheque every week." Sandi quit the hospital and worked for a physician who was setting up a cosmetic health care clinic. "It was challenging and interesting. I spent three years helping this physician develop his clinic." Then one Friday night the doctor handed her an envelope and said, "Here is two weeks' pay. It has been wonderful working with you. But I have decided to reorganise my offices and I no longer need your services." Sandi had just been separated from her husband for three months and now she had no job. "I was in shock."

With the help of a lawyer friend Sandi sued the physician who had fired her for no good reason. Totally demoralised she agreed to settle out of court with a decent severance. "That was the beginning of wonderful things happening. Even though it looked like a terrible thing."

Her settlement came at the height of the recession. "I thought, 'What am I going to do?' At that time there were no jobs in the hospitals, absolutely zero." Furthermore, aside from the severance pay, she was broke. "I had zero money. I had lived from pay cheque to pay cheque. I could pay my mortgage and feed my kids…but my kids never had pizza or cases of pop. That was just a luxury."

Now three years later, this entrepreneur has no idea how much money she makes. But she more than pays her bills. "I can do special things with my children. I put $7000 in my retirement plan, but this is the first time in my life that I have ever had the revenue to be able to do that." However, she does not measure her entrepreneurial success by money so much as the contentment within her soul and the balance she strives towards in her personal and business lives as she takes charge of her own journey.

On the first appointed afternoon, in the middle of a heavy January snowfall, I pulled up behind Sandi's Jeep in her front yard. We had not met, but had spoken on the telephone a number of times. A tall woman with short blond hair opens the door with a big affable smile, telling me that she just arrived home and has let her dog out for a run. Suddenly, as though she realizes her status as a professional woman, she stops, looks me straight in the eye, puts out her hand, and formally says, "How do you do?" While she oozes with confidence, she also exudes a warm receptive friendly attitude. For a few minutes Sandi takes time getting the dog back in, feeding him treats, and enjoying the home environment.

By 2:10 p.m. she settles in her downstairs work area at her large desk that sits in the corner of a large darkly lit recreation room. Her dining room table and chairs fill the centre of this downstairs room because she is redecorating her dining/living room. Her computer and fax machine sit on a little desk in the corner of another room that she refers to as the family room.

At 2:15 p.m. Sandi calls the dentist to cancel her son's appointment, which was set up today to coincide with a sales call she had scheduled nearby with a doctor. She has been trying to confirm the meeting with this doctor who wants a demonstration of her collagen product. But her messages have gone unanswered. The appointment was scheduled for 3:00 p.m.

After cancelling the dental appointment, she perseveres and makes one more call to the doctor's office asking for a response one way or another. It is not exactly a demanding voice, more of a commanding tone that requires an answer. While she waits for the return call she decides to run up to the kitchen to brew some coffee. She returns with a cup for each of us and a can of Pringles for lunch.

She talks excitedly about a management course she took this week. Evidently the seminar leader touched upon categorising sales calls. Sandi categorises the prospective sales call to the doctor as a "maybe" call because "he has been interested, but not terribly interested". It would not surprise her if he does not return the phone call today to confirm the appointment. Now she understands what the course facilitator meant by a "maybe" call being a waste of time. "Yes and no answers are the answers to spend time getting."

Since it seems she may have a free afternoon she decides to put the things she learned from the management course into action. First of all, she needs to straighten her desk. "The facilitator suggested that one's desk should be cleaned with only the telephone and your present project on the top of it." After clearing off her desk, she has a list of things to do, but has learned that she must prioritise what she should tackle.

When Sandi takes courses it seems she puts theory into action immediately. While out of work and in a depressed state, she applied and was accepted into an entrepreneurial program subsidised by the government. "It was wonderful. They were wonderful, wonderful people. All of us were very traumatised from loss of jobs and were wondering where to go. And they taught us everything from accounting to sales…to setting goals and being balanced." As soon as the five-week course finished, Sandi opened her business using all the knowledge gleaned from the course. "Nice thing…was that it allowed me to collect insurance for one year and try to earn money. It takes time to establish the business."

She confesses that while she did open her business, she did not really believe at the beginning that she would remain in business for herself. "I was scared to death. I had no idea where it was leading. I think I thought it was a stopgap between getting a full-time job, a real job. I think out of our class that was what most people did. They ended up thinking they had a business but really became employees because that is your safety net–to be employed…I think in my headspace I said, 'Sure I am going to give it a try and do some consulting work. But hopefully Charlie is going to hire me as a full-time nurse educator. I am going to get a doctor like I used to work for that will hire me on full time. I am not really going to be working for a bunch of different people. That's not gonna happen.'"

Prior to taking the entrepreneurial course, Sandi's emotional problems had culminated in her being diagnosed with acute depression. As an out patient she attended a daily psychiatric program, "which I really was very dependent upon." However, she submitted a resume and a business plan as part of her application for the entrepreneurial course. "They had about 125 applicants and they took 25 fortunate people for the class." She was one of the fortunate people accepted. When she shared this news with her psychiatrist she told him, "I've been able to get into this program. But I don't know if I can do it." It meant dropping out of the structured psychiatric program where someone was taking care of her. Her psychiatrist responded with, "Sandi, you are not crazy. You are just depressed. I think personally this program would be the best thing for you." Since then Sandi has confirmed that psychiatrist's opinion.

Today in her little office in the corner of the basement, the entrepreneur's phone rings. At 2:25 p.m. the doctor calls to confirm the 3:00 p m. meeting. Sandi opens a little white cabinet near her desk and takes out her collagen needles and places them into her briefcase. In two minutes she has her overcoat on and runs to her Jeep. She backs up around my car in the snow-covered driveway, confident of her driving skills. The unplowed roads do not concern her in the least.

On our way to the doctor's office she remembers when she did not ooze confidence. She had been fired. She had experienced the trauma of having to physically go to the office to sign up to collect insurance. "The girl who was interviewing me was just awful. I was humiliated. I was in tears. I remember writing a hate letter to my boss [who fired me] while I was sitting in the employment office."

By 3:05 p.m. Sandi arrives at the doctor's office. She takes a moment to apply lipstick and lip liner while still in the Jeep. "I always look my best, since I am in this business. People ask me all the time if I have it [collagen injections] done." She does.

As she walks towards the office, Sandi takes long confident strides in her full-length cloth coat, velvet black scarf, and her elegant, high boots. In the office she slips off her overcoat to reveal a short black jacket with buttons, a patterned blouse, and belted tan trousers. Upon speaking to the receptionist Sandi discovers that the doctor has booked off one hour for the sales call. The patient on whom Sandi will demonstrate the collagen treatment arrives just after us. Sandi had asked the receptionist to have the doctor put a numbing cream on the patient before Sandi's arrival because it takes one-half hour for the cream to work. Sandi expresses disappointment when she realises the patient has just walked in. Furthermore, she is not excited to learn that the patient is the doctor's wife.

We all enter an examining room. The patient expresses a desire for collagen infusion in her lips, as well as around her lips, and also discusses pain relievers. Sandi puts numbing cream on the patient's lips. The patient asks for Tylenol since she has had a similar procedure before and found it painful. Neither Sandi nor the doctor has any Tylenol.

While they wait for the numbing to take effect, Sandi discusses the newest product, which is a gel form. She capably lists all of its advantages. Furthermore, she explains that the collagen company is training doctors to demonstrate the product to their colleagues, indicating that there will be workshops in this area in the spring. Sandi wastes little time getting straight to the point by asking him when he would like to see these training sessions held.

While the physician ignores Sandi's question about training sessions, he counters with his own question about the length of time the injections last. Sandi immediately answers his query. She then discusses inventory and costs with the doctor, mentioning how to order the product in order to save on shipping costs. Throughout the demonstration, Sandi exhibits a professional, knowledgeable attitude.

Sandi hands the doctor sales brochures. "Voila!" she exclaims with a smile, indicating this is the end of her sales pitch.

Although the doctor barely nods as he takes the brochures, Sandi continues smiling and chatting. She asks the patient how much lip she wants and what she has had done.

Then Sandi turns her attention back to the physician mentioning his new office, about which he chats quite freely. Without missing her chance, Sandi suggests that he display some posters on collagen in both offices. He only nods.

Sandi asks the patient. "Are you ready?" While preparing to apply the injections Sandi chats about their children. "How are the kids doing?" The conversation leads into the fact that the doctor's children attend university.

Without missing a beat, Sandi laughs and says, "Next year I'll have two kids in university. That's why you have to buy this product from me. Help me out!" They all laugh.

Sandi's persistence in selling her product to this physician never flags. The doctor's negligible responses do not dampen her perseverance. She divulges later that she has not always been so comfortable approaching people. But she persevered over the last three years. Now she says, "I believe in the value of the service I provide and it is worth every penny!"

One of the first obstacles that she encountered when starting out on her entrepreneurial journey involved the whole notion of value. "Two men were totally demoralising. I remember going on a call with one of them one time and coming back from Niagara Falls. They were trying to see how I was doing because if I wasn't doing all that well then they could not pay me a whole lot. They really kind of put the gears into me…I was still not in great shape and I remember the tears. I had all these men around me trying to make me feel that I am not worth what I am asking."

She turned for help from the people running the entrepreneurial program. "I was introduced to one of their consultants who was retired from the medical business. He was wonderful. He made me ask for what I was worth. One of the hardest things to do is ask for money. I was constantly in environments where people were trying to make me feel that I was not worth what I was asking. That was a huge hurdle."

Today in this doctor's little office Sandi's main concern lies in making the patient comfortable without the proper equipment and lighting to carry out the collagen treatment. They finally settle on having the patent sit in a normal arm chair while her husband, the doctor, holds her head so she is not too uncomfortable.

Sandi shows genuine regard for the woman's comfort throughout the treatment. "You're comfortable on the chair? Occasionally she calls out "pinch" to the woman to indicate the injection will hurt. When the patient winces, Sandi stops injecting long enough to ask, "Are you ok?"

When the patient starts moving a little, Sandi steps away, giving her time to re-adjust and says, "Just tell me when."

Sandi discusses the technique with the doctor. "This is how we stretch the lip. We're missing some right there." By 4:07 p.m. she has completed injecting inside and around the lips. She applies Polysporin to clean the lips, and explains to the patient that it will take a week or two to get used to the larger lips. "Just like it takes awhile to get accustomed to a new hair do!"

"I like her lips!" Sandi exclaims as she stands back to assess her job. Once again she takes the opportunity to promote her product. "It takes a little more time with zyderm, but it's worth it." The patient indicates that it hurts as Sandi continues to make a few more injections. "Do you want a little in the middle?"

Now it is time to let the patient look in mirror to decide. Tears appear on the patient's cheeks. "Oops tears–tears of joy!" Sandi exclaims, turning a negative into a positive. Then in a reassuring tone, Sandi says, "The lips will settle. Give it two hours. While continuing to discuss technique with the doctor, Sandi does not forget to include the patient. She looks at the patient's lips and says, "Very nice actually."

When the woman indicates that she feels a lump on the inside of her lip, Sandi immediately stops talking with the doctor, puts on rubber gloves, and feels inside her lip. She confirms that it is a lump of collagen that "tracked down". Sandi assures her that the lump will disappear in a week.

Sandi packs her briefcase, says goodbye, and leaves quickly. While she persevered in her sales pitch and demonstrated the treatment whole-heartedly, this saleswoman recognises that she will not be receiving large orders from this office. She turns to me in the Jeep and says, "It was a bit of a waste of time to drive all this way in the snow." Sandi discloses to me that she knows the doctor only wants the product to inject his own wife.

It was obvious to this entrepreneur who has come a long way in her journey that the physician knew he was only interested in buying enough supplies for his wife before Sandi ever entered his office. Nevertheless, Sandi took the opportunity to give him her sales pitch while waiting for the freezing to occur and during the treatment she had promised to provide. She remained friendly and informative throughout, demonstrating how she won top honors in the sales department for the collagen company. "For the very first time, the company decided in July to have a bonus given for the two top sales representatives, not for the total sales achieved, but the highest percentage over your forecast. You are given a forecast and a budget. I don't know numbers but I ended up top international...I was shocked! I only get paid for two days that I work for [the company] and all the other people are paid a salary plus a percentage for their sales. They get paid if they make the quota and a percentage over that. I mean there's no incentive for me to go crazy...I get a pretty average salary...It is not high. It is not low. It is fair."

It is not the money she makes as a sales representative that keeps her working for this company. "When they asked me to do it, it was a six-month maternity leave for two days a week. I said 'I'll take the job. I'll do it for nothing because of the contacts.' I'm in touch with every dermatologist and plastic [surgeon] in my area. This is my business. This is fabulous."

Sandi demonstrates her understanding of the power of networking as she continues to discuss her position as a sales representative in the collagen company. "This was a huge way [to move my business forward]. And they were actually going to pay me every day to do this...You see it wasn't the dollar that drew me to that job. It was the contacts and the networking. And the money was a bonus!"

As soon as she began her unique consulting business just over three years ago, she started to network. "I realised that because of my business relationship with the physician I had worked with I also had different laser companies where I knew the guys well. So I put out feelers." Later when she reflects on how her consulting operation has flourished in three short years she attributes it to one main reason. "It was my networking that helped me build my business."

In addition to understanding the concept of networking, Sandi also knew that a businessperson must find a specific niche that needs to be filled. "I think in many business relationships you have to have something that that person does not have. And they are providing something for you. That way it works." So when Sandi sent out feelers to the physicians she would say, 'Why don't you hire me as a consultant. [I'll] come and help you sell these lasers and show physicians when they get these lasers how to use them, how to set up the office for them, how to train their staff." She knew from her own experience that if the physicians bought the lasers they needed the training. "I was working in an office where we bought a laser, and when it showed up on the doorstep none of us knew how to use it!"

On her way home today she checks her voice mail messages and listens to them in the car. She likes to makes full use of her time, although she is considering buying a speakerphone for the car for more safety. With the last phone call her business day is complete. I will meet with her the next afternoon as she takes on the role of health consultant.

Upon her arrival at home, her son meets her at the door. They immediately fall into a conversation about their respective days. It is easy to recognise the rapport mother and offspring have. In a later conversation with me she discusses the balance she maintains between her personal and business life. She knows she could move her business forward faster if that was her goal. However, pushing her business ahead and making lots of money do not top her list of goals. "My priority is my children. I think if I were a single woman with no dependants I would move my business forward. I think there is a big need for nurses with my skills and I could have easily set up training programs to train nurses…Almost like a head hunter, but with the specialty of cosmetic health care. I thought about it one time…But I think where I am and I have had a multitude of opportunities presented to me with a lot of people offering me full time work…that would be fine if I didn't have children, but I do have children. Maybe in five years time I will want to do that."

Achieving a balance in her life has proven difficult since she left the safety net of the hospital seven years ago. She admits that being fired and going through the depths of depression led her to books on spirituality.

For example, Sarah Ban Breathnach's *Simple Abundance* made her realise what is important in her life. "Maybe what happens when you become self employed is you do get kind of greedy. I think that can happen sometimes. You start making money and you want more. It is just not what motivates me and yet I need money to live. I am not pretending that I am rich. I am not rich, but happy with my lifestyle."

She shares the notion that she wants her own children to find balance in their lives too. For example, she talks about her oldest child in university. "My daughter has a student loan and I was hesitant about her applying for it. I wanted her to try to do it without going that route. But then I sort of thought about it and said, "You know it is teaching her a lot of responsibility." As Sandi has moved towards reaching a balance between making enough money without being greedy on her entrepreneurial journey and maintaining a home life she feels she has blossomed as a human being that is happy and contented with her life.

It is the next afternoon that provides an environment for this entrepreneur to display just how much she has blossomed as a human being. We have made arrangements to meet at 12:30 p.m. in the cosmetic surgeon's office where she works as an aesthetic health care consultant/laser specialist. The dimmed lights, mirrored closet doors, lush plants, and thick carpet in the elegant reception area indicates expensive services. The friendly receptionist sits at a desk behind a window that she opens to address the clients in the waiting room.

Sandi is standing behind the receptionist talking on the telephone, but immediately hangs up, and comes around through a door to greet me with her friendly smile and warm handshake. "Come on through." I walked through a door leading into the hallway that in turn led to the various offices and examining rooms.

Sandi's outfit reflects the elegant setting in a medical office. She wears belted black wool slacks, flat black loafers, a lacy black velvet blouse and a purple mohair cardigan. Over this she wore a white lab coat.

By 12:42 p.m. Sandi enthusiastically shows me binders filled with before and after shots of faces, eyes, lips, tummy tucks, and thighs. She describes the wonderful skin care program they introduce to their patients. "The entire staff is on the program, even the male surgeon. It is so good that we do not use moisturiser except in the winter."

As she introduces me to the staff and walks through the office area, Sandi appears comfortable and contented with her environment. Later she tells me that it was not until she started with the surgeon who runs this clinic that she felt she was worth what she was asking. She had been told by the two men who had driven home from Niagara Falls with her that this surgeon had spoken to them and said that he would not pay her half of what she felt her services were worth. However, she persevered and met with the surgeon anyway. "I went and presented what I wanted on an hourly basis, a re-evaluation in a year on a percentage basis. They needed me and I needed them. It was a win/win situation for both of us!" For Sandi this marked the turning point in her entrepreneurial endeavours. She knew she was worth what she was asking and went out to find more consulting work in the surrounding area where she discovered additional win/win circumstances.

Sandi greets the first patient of the afternoon with a smile and a hand-shake, while exuding the joy and satisfaction of a winner. Before starting the treatment, she ensures that the patient does not mind my being in attendance in this large white examination room. She is constantly aware of the patient's contentment. For example, she re-adjusts the big dentist-like chair in the middle of the room by moving it up and down slightly by touching the buttons with her foot until the patient is at a comfortable angle. She turns to me and says, "This is a real chair to use to work on a patient, unlike the chair I had to use in the office yesterday. Those premises were primitive by comparison." Clearly this consultant likes to have excellent equipment with which to work. As she reaches for a light that swivels like that used by dentists, she remarks, "We have great lighting here!"

Sandi skilfully injects the collagen in the woman's upper lip. She completes the task quickly and inquires whether the patient wants make up applied to cover the redness that occurs after the injections. After carefully covering the redness with foundation herself, Sandi suggests that the lady apply her own lipstick in the washroom. The client leaves, smiling at both Sandi and I.

By 1:05 p.m. Sandi meets with the second patient in Sandi's tiny well-appointed office. Her framed degrees and certificates hang on beautiful dark green wallpapered walls providing patients with a sense of well being that they are being taken care of by a trained professional. Sandi asks how the patient is doing from her last visit. Then she looks closely at the woman's face and shoulders to observe the healing. "How are you today? What are we doing today?" She injects some saline solution into a few of the shoulder veins before deciding to do laser treatment on the remaining veins. They must walk upstairs one floor above to a very small examination room to carry out the laser treatment.

Once the patient is settled on the examination table with the large dentist-like lamp attached, Sandi shows genuine concern for the patient because she had injected the salt water without a painkiller. While the patient does not seem to mind, Sandi insists that they try an experiment. She wipes numbing cream on the patient's one shoulder and holds a pack of ice on the other shoulder to freeze it. Before beginning the laser treatment Sandi provides us with laser protective glasses, and asks the patient, "Are you comfy?" This laser specialist uses a foot pedal to move the table exactly in position, and swings the lamp over the patient's shoulder. When it comes to performing these techniques Sandi is a perfectionist. For example, throughout the surgery she comments on the fact that the light is too tight to adjust correctly. Yet she does not forget that she is working on a patient who is wide-awake. When she finds it hot in the room Sandi takes off her lab coat, but asks the patient, "Are you cold since you are half-naked and we are so hot?" The patient has removed her top so that Sandi can perform the laser treatment on her shoulders. She also chats continuously to the woman about movies, the weather, etc. However, when asked about the laser technology, Sandi's responds knowledgeably in a professional manner.

When the patient indicates that she does not feel pain in the shoulder that had the cream applied, Sandi changes from pulse mode to continuous mode because it is faster and easier. "I was worried about putting too much cream on because I did not want to ruin your clothes should it seep into the sweater later on." With the treatment completed, Sandi explains to the patient what to expect throughout the healing process before saying goodbye and rushing to her next appointment downstairs.

It is now 1:55 p.m. and this patient has waited since 1:30 p.m. Sandi apologises and ushers her into the large treatment room quickly. They immediately begin discussing the patient's varicose veins. Sandi looks at the legs and listens carefully to her explanation of having another surgeon remove her larger veins but refusing to remove her spider veins. Sandi summarises the patient's tale before moving on to discuss her history of thrombosis. Sandi will not do any injections at this time, but lists the woman's options. "You could see another surgeon upstairs before we do anything or we could just do the spider veins and see what happens, or do nothing." Although she indicates concern over the woman's well being, she laughs at her third option.

When the patient discloses that her mother had varicose veins, Sandi laughs in a friendly way. "Your are cooked!" Always the professional though, Sandi continues to take notes about the patient's history and specifics. Sandi then insists that the patient consult with the in-house surgeon in her office. "I think you could get good cosmetic results but I would like to make sure everything is good." The woman finally agrees and Sandi immediately finds the surgeon and leaves the two of them to chat awhile. When he reports back to Sandi that the patient really should see another surgeon to check things out, Sandi returns to the patient. "I'd feel better if you'd see him first. The girls in the front will get an appointment for you. Just come around to the front and we'll do that for you."

At 2:30 p.m. Sandi meets with the surgeon, the general manager (the surgeon's wife), and an aesthetician. Sandi opens the meeting. "We need to find where an aesthetician fits in the office." They discuss the current makeup they use as Sandi provides samples for the aesthetician. They discuss skin care pre and post operatively. "We want a product that will give the patient good coverage, but not heavy coverage." Sandi enthusiastically suggests setting up binders filled with pictures. "There is so much we can do, and explore." The aesthetician agrees and indicates that she would enjoy doing the exploring. The surgeon needs to leave for an appointment but the meeting continues. Sandi suggests how the aesthetician could be part of the team. But before showing her a small room on the first floor of the medical building where she could have her practice, they discuss financial options with this entrepreneur.

After the struggles Sandi has had with the financial side of her entrepreneurial business, she is now in a position where she feels worthy but feels compassion for other entrepreneurs. Later Sandy shares how her attitude changed once she believed that her services were worth what she was asking. For example, one of her part-time consulting jobs was really not worth the contractual fee she was receiving because of the time it took her to drive into the city. She wrote the surgeon a letter describing her situation and stating that her fee would now be a 60/40 split. "He freaked. He went nuts! I didn't care. I didn't need the job…Before I would have put up with this [situation]. But now I am in a different situation where if I don't like it, I can leave because I have a million other things to work with."

While Sandi runs a consulting business that more than pays her bills now, she does not make money her main priority. She admits, "I am not a numbers person." People she has worked with in the past seem to put most of their emphasis on making money. "It wouldn't matter if they made $500,000 or a million and a half dollars, it would never be enough…I just feel differently." She confesses that perhaps part of the reason is that she simply never had enough money to worry about managing.

But then she adds, "I think I don't know how to manage money but I think I do. I obviously do or I wouldn't be where I am!"

Sandi hires an accountant for her business. However, they continuously cancel appointments to work on the books. She confides that when she took the priority management course she decided that meeting with her accountant regularly must become a priority. "I give her everything and she looks after it. I do my own invoicing and my son helps me a lot with that. It is not something I enjoy doing at all!"

Meanwhile, she certainly does enjoy consulting with patients. After showing the aesthetician her new office, Sandi returns to her own office where she greets a male patient who had a facial treatment and returns for a check-up. They discuss his skin care program, along with specific tanning products he can use. She even shows him the amount of sunscreen to use. She must be very positive with him. She turns to me and says, "He was at the 'I hate it stage' before this. He is beginning to like the look now." He asks for more free samples of the skin care product. "You're not on a medical plan are you?" She grabs a handful of samples for him before he leaves the office.

At 4:02 p.m. Sandi quickly ushers another patient into the office. "Are you feeling more comfortable?" She looks at the patient's face carefully before pulling out the file with the before pictures. She compares the pictures to the patient's face today. She asks about the patient's routine. She makes suggestions. "Use sun fader every morning!"

The patient asks Sandi about her daughter's skin. Sandi immediately gives her a sample of a different product for the teen to use, along with very specific directions. "Now let's take your picture!" Sandi swiftly walks out of the office, and just as quickly returns with a camera. She snaps the picture. "Fabulous! Let me just chart it!" Sandi wastes no time suggesting a follow-up appointment in eight weeks unless the patient has any trouble before then. "Goodbye. Bring your daughter in next time!"

Sandi exudes confidence in her work as a consultant, in her relationship with each patient. Yet before embarking on her entrepreneurial venture she had no idea what to do. When asked if she had ever dreamed of being an entrepreneur, she does not hesitate to answer. "Absolutely not! I lost my job, and I ended up with no alternative. I ended up with one door closing, but one opening."

It was her lawyer who served the papers on her former boss who actually put the idea of being an entrepreneur in her head. He asked her one day, "How many people do what you do?" She responded with, "Well probably nobody because my boss opened the first office that involved a lot of laser cosmetic stuff." Her lawyer responded with, "Why don't you go out on your own and start your own business?" Sandi's immediate thought was, "Are you stupid? No, no, no. I am a nurse…People tell me what to do. And I grew up in a very structured environment!"

Sandi's interest in becoming an entrepreneur piqued when she read an article in the newspaper about a nurse manager. "She had lost her job and had decided to become an entrepreneurial consultant." Then through a chance meeting with a woman in the waiting room at the unemployment office Sandi learned about the entrepreneurial program offered in her own town that she eventually joined.

One of the main hurdles she faced once she decided to become an entrepreneur was obtaining a loan to begin the business. She needed $2500 from the bank to get started. "I was dealing with this bank manager. He was terrible to me…I didn't have major debts other than my house. But this man would not give me a loan. Would not! I was so upset…It was another hit on my self-esteem…I went back to that man twice and he kept stringing me along. Instead of just saying 'no I am not going to do it,' he made me come back two or three times. I found it so humiliating."

Eventually she changed banks and by re-negotiating her mortgage through a female loans officer in another bank she received the necessary money for her business. "[This loans officer] was very interested in my business and what I did…She wanted to do collagen. I faxed her all of the information!"

Back in her office today, she displays no concern about money. She is a busy entrepreneur who loves it. "I like the variety. I think that is what keeps me motivated to grow. I like working as a clinician and learning lasers and technique. But yet I'm doing some sales, which I never thought I would do. But that's going to lead me to an educational position maybe down the road. I like the variety."

By 4:10 p.m. Sandi is taking a before picture of the next client. The first question this patient has concerns the cost and Sandi addresses it with a straightforward attitude. They move on to discuss the woman's family history, allergies, health, etc. The patient expresses a desire to have the treatment this afternoon but is concerned about the late hour so suggests that Sandi not use the cream that takes one half hour to freeze the area. Sandi assures her that she has the time to wait for the numbing cream. As she is rubbing the cream on the patient, the woman comments on how much more thorough Sandi is than a previous doctor had been. Sandi responds very professionally. "Well, we all do things differently." Sandi continues to provide her with information about the treatment. "Use sunscreen. If you don't you're wasting your money." The treatment costs $300. With that Sandi tells the patient to enjoy the background music while the cream takes effect. "I'll be back!"

At 4:30 p.m. Sandi apologises to the next patient who had been waiting as she ushers her into a well appointed little room in the back. They sit at a beautiful round wooden table with silk flowers on it. Sandi listens intently to the client's problem, while writing down the medical history. She is very personable in this first consultation, providing personal illustrations. For example, with a pleasant, friendly smile she tries to convince the young woman to stop smoking by telling her a little story.

Sandi asks the woman to describe exactly what she wants changed about her face and charts it on a diagram of a face. They discuss the skin care system she and her colleagues believe in and Sandi explain how it would work on the patient's skin without any other treatment. She shows the patient a binder filled with before and after pictures of patients who have followed this particular skin care program. She also informs her of the cost involved. The woman expresses a great deal of interest so Sandi suggests that the patient watch a three-minute video describing the program. She sets the video up and leaves the patient while checking on her other patient.

It is now 5:05 p.m. The office is officially closed, but Sandi will complete the treatment for the one patient and provide the skin care products for the second patient before leaving the clinic for the day. The afternoon has been back-to-back appointments, but she will leave within a half-hour.

Sandi strives to live the balanced life she studied during her entrepreneurial course. "Being self employed allows you to gain self control in your life. You can work like a crazy woman or you can just work at the pace that you need to work at." She believes that fear of not having enough money drives the entrepreneur to work long hours. "But when you have that fear, and this is something that I have learned, it really does inhibit you from doing your job well." She has learned to get over the fear. She now commands her own future. There seems no end to this woman's entrepreneurial journey. When asked to work full time for someone else she emphatically refuses. "I wouldn't do it. You couldn't pay me enough to do it!"

For Sandi the goal of an entrepreneur should not be about riches. "You reach that comfort level that money is not the be all and end all. You know, it doesn't always buy you the security you are after. What buys you a happy life is being balanced and having faith in yourself."

CHAPTER FIVE

▼

THE HOLISTIC PATTERN

Amy, Barbara, Sandi, and Diane each tell their own story, yet woven in and out of the intricate details emerges a similar holistic pattern of three major elements in the four separate experiences. Clearly, in the decision-making stage to enter the entrepreneurial journey, each woman had certain personal characteristics that helped them in the opening of their enterprise. Each of them found that certain contextual elements emerged that provided them with a purpose for being on the venture. Finally, they found that specific operational elements contributed to their respective decisions for continuing or terminating the journey.

Beginning the Journey: Personal Elements in Place

All four entrepreneurs brought a range of personal strengths and circumstances to their respective businesses that enabled them to open and manage their particular ventures. Common strengths and circumstances included a specific skill set, attitudes, personality traits and sociological conditions. For each of the women, these four categories combined to create a desire to begin a new venture.

Skills

Technical skills means that the entrepreneurs understood their product or services, had the ability to design or redesign the business, and had a good knowledge of the industry. All four women had had some technical skill prior to starting their journey as an entrepreneur, and continued to work on skills once in the business. While Amy attended Coffee College and Diane enrolled in journalism class, Sandi and Barbara had had on-the-job training.

Amy, a former nurse, bought a coffee shop franchise with high standards, grueling training, and tests. While the franchise had originally helped her open and design the shop, after one and a half years in the franchise business, she understood enough to tell me, "I wouldn't franchise again". On the other hand, Barbara and Sandi had both been employed in their respective industries prior to striking out on their own. Barbara followed industry trends by reading trade magazines and attending seminars. Sandi had trained in a cosmetic surgeon's clinic for three years, and as a freelance saleswoman, had "ended up top international sales representative" with the collagen company. Meanwhile, Diane "decided to do freelancing [writing] and at the same time I enrolled in magazine journalism." Diane learned that writing was a competitive business, but she cut a niche for herself in the commercial market by specializing in corporate communications, in addition to writing magazine articles.

The women demonstrated human skills by their understanding of how to lead and motivate employees and how to network with people outside of the business. All four women were involved with people every day from the beginning of their journeys. Their human skills were evident in the observations and the interviews.

When Barbara opened her own shop she hired a friend to work for her. She ignored the guidelines for hiring staff that she had learned from her experiences. She wound up having to fire two employees before finding two great replacements. Amy got it right from the beginning. When asked if she put her staff ahead of her customers, Amy replied, "I do set them above my customers…I care." While Sandi did not employ anyone, she knew how to network. "It was my networking that helped me build my business." Amongst other things, Diane networked with a writing group, took an active role, and set up a website to promote the writing group. When Barbara first opened her store she joined a breakfast networking group "that helped a little bit but I just found out that the place where I was most productive…was being in the store because I've made some great contacts with people just being in here." Amy worked the street, smiling and waving at everyone when she walked through town. She was simply part of the community and known as the coffee shop owner.

The businesswomen demonstrated their administrative skills through detailed planning. While the skill sets varied in the management of their businesses, the four women all indicated that an important aspect of administering the business was managing finances. Sandi postponed dealing with financial concerns, while Barbara emphasized their importance. Diane routinely set aside time to do the accounting, and Amy worried about the lack of good management on the part of the franchiser.

Amy had learned how to plan and manage her shop so well that after 18 months she was critical of the franchise's inept administrative abilities. For example, "I think the advertising is the pits at this franchise…that is where we lose a lot." Sandi questioned her administrative skills, so she attended a priority management course, where she realized she must meet with her accountant frequently. "It really is something that weighs on me, and something I have learned in the last year is that I tend to be a bit of a procrastinator." On the other hand, Diane did her own books, managing finances with little trouble. She routinely marked her time on the time sheet throughout the day, so she could easily invoice clients later. Barbara excelled in administrative skills, as illustrated when she created a business plan in a self-employment assistance program.

Attitudes

Each of the women held an uncompromising outlook on life as an entrepreneur. Three common attitudes, or outlooks, shared by everyone of them included drive, persistence, and acceptance of working under ambiguous circumstances.

They demonstrated their drive simply by being motivated enough to start and continue to be on the entrepreneurial journey for at least eighteen months. By their own admission, both Amy and Barbara were driven. Amy had a desire to give 100% in everything. "When I take things on, be it at home or here, it really is all or nothing." For Barbara, "it was something I had to do."

When asked what continued to motivate her to remain on the journey twelve years later, Diane laughed as she described family expenses, but added, "I do get a lot of satisfaction out of doing the work. I do enjoy it." Sandi demonstrated her motivation by her obvious enjoyment when she showed me a photo album filled with pictures of satisfied patients after their cosmetic surgery. She was motivated by the recognition she received as sales representative of the year. Before describing the award, she asked, "Am I supposed to blow my own horn?" These women did not need an external force to get them to work. Their motivation came from within. It was intrinsic, not extrinsic.

Persistence in these women was evident as perseverance or determination in both beginning the entrepreneurial journey and continuing in it despite some setbacks they had not anticipated. Amy acknowledged the challenges she faces daily. "This is a hell of a job. I had no idea—it is physical, it is a mental kind of thing. You think, 'Oh good—almost caught up'—yet there are twenty other things that need to be done. If they are not done, you have a problem tomorrow."

Both Barbara and Sandi demonstrated persistence when dealing with bank loan managers. When faced with having to repay a large bank loan, Barbara refused to declare bankruptcy, secured another loan from a different bank and made the payment. "I won't [give in]. No matter what…if it is something that means the life of my business—I fight tooth and nail." For Sandi who was just starting her journey, getting a loan from one bank proved humiliating and useless. Nevertheless, she approached another bank where she secured a start up loan.

For these four, persistence to overcome the obstacles was critical to starting their journey, as well as continuing it once operational. It may not have been easy to carry on, yet each entrepreneur did so. Whether it was getting a bank loan or dealing with physical exhaustion, they all persevered.

Ambiguity for the entrepreneurs meant being uncertain because of the constant and unpredictable changes in the entrepreneurial journey. For Amy, ambiguity was a way of life for an entrepreneur. Initially, Sandi found the ambiguous situation intolerable when she lost her job. However, three years later, she looked forward to whatever the future brings. "I like the variety!" For Barbara, ambiguity meant "lots of options. I love change. I don't like being stagnant." Like Barbara, Diane was thrilled by ambiguity because there is the element of the chase.

Each of these women knew they had to tolerate ambiguity, if they were to continue the journey. Although there was no guaranteed pay cheque, the majority of them even experienced a certain thrill about future possibilities.

Personality Traits

While each of the four women had a different personality, there were two traits common to all: creativity and innovation. Interestingly, the two traits were so intertwined in each of them that where there was creativity, there was also innovation.

The entrepreneurs demonstrated the existence of a creative trait when they could visualize changes or transformations within their businesses. They illustrated their innovative trait when they could put the changes or transformations into action. Each of the four entrepreneurs would think about an idea and then act upon it.

For Amy, people were her "raison d'être," and it was her handling of people that highlighted both her creative and innovative traits. When she opened her store she had a lot of applicants that she simply could not interview, so she sent each one a personal letter of appreciation. "I included a 'treat-a-friend' card that asked them to please come on in to the store. Ask for Amy and introduce yourselves." Sandi wanted to change her business relationship with one of the surgeons by either increasing her consulting fees or not having to travel to his clinic. When he declined her new fee structure, it freed Sandi from the contract with him and allowed her to travel elsewhere.

Both Barbara and Diane illustrated creativity in thinking of ways to meet the client's expectations, and innovativeness in making the expectation a reality. Barbara told the story about one of her customers. "She had a 20-foot window. We had absolutely no supplier that could supply a wrought iron rod that was 20 feet long. You can't ship it; you can't forge it; you can't do anything with it. So we had to figure out a way. Their brackets didn't work. So we ended up using what is usually a hold back for brackets and we filed them down and modified the whole thing and joined it all…It was worth thousands and thousands of dollars."

Meanwhile, as a magazine writer, Diane has to "come up with the idea first and then present it [the idea] to the editor." She then must be innovative enough to "come up with a solution!" When she suggested an article on home births, she "wrote about when Carrie [my daughter] was born."

In all four women, the innovative trait followed very closely behind the creative trait as they continued in their entrepreneurial journey. But these innate traits were definitely part of their individual personalities before any of them had embarked on their respective ventures.

Sociological Conditions

Sociological conditions played a role in their decision to begin the entrepreneurial journey. Gender was naturally a condition in this journey. Educational backgrounds were similar, as were ages. But there were some surprises with respect to childhood backgrounds.

The educational background of the four women was surprisingly similar. All four had received their undergraduate degrees, although only Barbara had majored in business, with some preparatory entrepreneurial classes. Sandi and Amy had nursing degrees, and Diane held an arts degree. In addition, all four women had also taken steps towards preparing for their specific journeys into entrepreneurship. To learn how to open and manage a franchised coffee shop, Amy "did a month in coffee college" with her franchise. Both Barbara and Sandi prepared to begin their respective entrepreneurial journeys by taking the self-employment assistance course offered by the government. As for Diane, she wanted to make a career change so she enrolled in a college magazine journalism course. A specific educational background turned out to be a component that played a role in starting the journey.

The age at which the women either began the entrepreneurial journey or began to investigate the possibility of such a journey was, again, surprisingly consistent. Three of them were in their early 30's when they began to seriously contemplate an entrepreneurial venture. Amy said, "I was probably about 30, 31, 32. I started investigating businesses. You know again, younger kids—so that prevents you from doing what you want." Diane's response was similar. "I guess I was 30, 29, 30." Barbara knew exactly when she made the decision to start her shop. "I was 34. I think 35 was a milestone for me because I thought even in my 20's I would have my own business...So the 35 looming was, I think, kind of a milestone. I turned 35 about 6 months after I started the business." At 44, Sandi was older than the other three women were when she opened her business, although the age differential is relatively small. Age was an interesting similarity and another component in the decision to begin the entrepreneurial journey.

Childhood background involves the degree to which the four women had any exposure to entrepreneurial activity in their formative years. Amy grew up in a family business. "My father was self-employed for 50 years, maybe 55 years. He sold out in June, and sold out as a self-made millionaire, and I thought that would probably be the route." Like Amy, Barbara's father had his own business for years. "And my grandmother was a designer in a large city…So maybe that is where the sewing thing comes from." Yet Sandi had nobody in her background who would be deemed entrepreneurial. Neither did Diane. Her father remained with one company. When asked if her mother had been entrepreneurial, Diane answered, "My mother? No." Half of these businesswomen had entrepreneurial families to model, while the other half had no such models.

All four women had a specific set of skills, attitudes, personality traits, and sociological conditions that proved important to them prior to even beginning their entrepreneurial journey. These elements are analogous to the items one would pack when planning a journey, most of which are probably readily available, but if not, may need to be procured. Most of the personal elements the aspiring entrepreneur may already possess, but some may have to be procured through some training. The packed items will go on the trip, just as the skills, attitudes, personality traits, and sociological conditions will still be part of the entrepreneurial journey once the business is opened.

Amy, Barbara, Sandi, and Diane demonstrated skills required to begin and to continue the entrepreneurial journey. Even Amy, who initially depended on the franchise for information and design, had learned a lot about running her business and was almost as proficient in her industry as the other three were in their respective fields. Their people skills were well honed; all four continuously networked outside of their businesses, while Amy and Barbara also worked at maintaining good staff relations. They all demonstrated detailed planning ability, and acknowledged that "the bottom line" was a good indication of excellent business management.

These women displayed similar attitudes both when they began and as they continued in their respective journeys. While Amy and Barbara admitted to being completely driven from the outset, Diane and Sandi indicated that their drive increased as they made profits and enjoyed the entrepreneurial journey. Without persistence, Diane would not have been admitted into journalism class, and Sandi would not have received the bank loan to start up. For Amy and Barbara, their persevering attitude allowed them to remain open despite setbacks such as long hours and bank managers calling in loans. All of them acknowledged that ambiguity was part of the entrepreneurial journey, and three of them believed that the ambiguity could actually be enjoyable.

Creativity and innovation were two personality traits common to all four from the beginning of their entrepreneurial journeys. Each of them had described a creative idea, and then discussed how they made it a reality in their business. By combining the two traits, they had designed a 'treat-a-friend' coupon, made a curtain rod out of pipes, left an undesired business relationship, or wrote a promised article.

The sociological elements were important components that lead them to begin their entrepreneurial journeys. Each of them had an undergraduate degree and had taken some form of preparatory training to start their respective journeys. Amy and Diane opened their businesses in their early thirties. Barbara opened her business just 6 months before the age of 35. Sandi began her journey at the age of 44, which was still within a relatively short span of 10 years from the other three women. It was a surprise to discover that only Amy and Barbara had entrepreneurial parents.

Continuing the Journey: Contextual Elements

The contextual elements included those aspects of the journey by which the women derived a sense of meaning about their experience. The contextual elements that surfaced included impetus for beginning the journey, personal control, outcomes of the journey, and sustainability of the journey. These specific conditions can fuse together to encourage or discourage the entrepreneur along the way.

Impetus

An impetus, or incentive, for beginning the journey continued to have its hold on the entrepreneurs once they had begun their respective businesses. However, the impetus took two different paths. Two of them felt pulled, or compelled, to become entrepreneurs, while the other two experienced more of a push into the world of the entrepreneur.

The motivating factor for both Amy and Barbara to begin their journeys was a "pull" that lured them into this entrepreneurial activity. While Amy waited until an appropriate time in her family's life to buy a franchise it was something that she had always considered doing. Barbara flatly dismissed a job offer worth six figures to continue with her entrepreneurial plans. "There was no stopping me!"

On the other hand, for Diane and Sandi, the motivating factor was more like a "push" to start their journeys. Both of them had received their degrees, obtained jobs, and did not think of entrepreneurial activities. In fact, Sandi said, "Did I want to be an entrepreneur? Absolutely not!" Although her lawyer suggested that she open her own laser consulting business, Sandi admits, "I ended up in the hospital in an out-patient basis classified as having acute depression." Then she read the nurse's article on being a consultant. Eventually she found herself in an entrepreneurial course where she discovered, "What most people fear—what drives people—to…work well at a job is fear of not having enough money…I was scared to death." Then she experienced a somewhat celestial push. "I got very spiritual. I read Deepak Chopra and a lot of really self-motivating things on positive thinking." She opened her consulting business. Three years later she is thriving both spiritually and financially.

At 30, Diane worked at a job she disliked. But it was her mother's death that pushed her into seriously considering what she did like and to go for it. She quit her job, and began writing part-time. Furthermore, she was pushed into full time entrepreneurship "4 ½ or 5 yeas ago when my husband wasn't working."

Personal Control

While their motivation for starting the journey may have differed amongst the four women, once they had begun their journey, each valued the second contextual element: personal control. They enjoyed having control over their own destinies.

After running clinics and doctors' offices for years, Amy had decided, "Enough is enough…working for everybody else 22 hours a day wasn't what I wanted to do any longer." It was time to take control, to be her own boss. Similarly, Barbara mentioned, "I had always wanted my own business for years and years. I had always thought about it while working for other people and decided at the end of my last job that the time was right." She later added, "There is so much freedom in your own business."

While Sandi had never harboured aspirations of owning a business, three years after being fired and running her own consulting enterprise, she confided, "I have control over my destiny now!" Similarly, Diane appreciates working in her own home, harbouring no intentions of working for anyone else, anywhere else.

Once the four women had been "pushed" or "pulled" into starting their individual entrepreneurial journeys, all enjoyed having a sense of personal control.

Outcomes

The third contextual element was the outcome, or result, of their chosen journeys. The outcomes emerged as each story unfolded. One outcome that was surprisingly similar in all four narratives was the excellent service each provided in their chosen venture. Another outcome that proved to be different for the women was their profitability in their chosen journeys.

One outcome observed in the women's journeys was the excellent service each provided daily. Amy's customers delighted in her attention and friendliness. She often listened to their stories while serving them. "I find it really amazing for 5 minutes when I get to talk to them what they tell me. It surprises me because I normally wouldn't tell a soul things like this—but they do…they will tell me their wife died three weeks ago. And I am around the corner [of the counter] and sitting down for 45 minutes." Amy demonstrated a caring personality throughout the observation day, and when asked about memorable moments in her business career, Amy regaled with stories of customers. "One customer, pregnant at the time…we were picking out patterns for the nursery."

As a clinician, Sandi also demonstrated that she cared for her clients. During collagen injections, she would ask, "How are you doing? OK." After taking the medical history of the patient with varicose veins, she insisted that she see a surgeon. For the man who initially hated the results of facial surgery, she demonstrated genuine empathy. Further, she encouraged those who were doing well and looking great by taking their pictures.

While Barbara greeted her customers in a friendly way, her approach was not so much one of caring but rather one of deciphering what the customer was looking for in the way of window covering. "You have to peg the customer and go from there. So you know you have to figure out what your customer wants." For example, when an elderly gentleman returned samples, Barbara understood that he wanted to come back with his wife before ordering, so she told him when she would be on the floor next time. Later, reflecting on the recession, Barbara acknowledged her customers' concerns about ordering merchandise from her for fear that she may not be in business. "Customers ask, 'Are you going to be here next year? Are you going to be here next week?'…They are a little gun-shy now. They don't want to give you money unless they are really sure you are going to be around. So it is important to preserve your image with the clients."

Diane approached the concept of serving her clients with a business-like attitude. The survey she sent to clients indicated they were satisfied which made her feel successful. Diane also indicated that when she took vacations she made alternative arrangements for her clients, usually with other writers. In the unusual circumstance of the ice storm, Diane demonstrated concern when she spoke to some of the victims. After the bulletin was circulated,

Diane remarked, "The people in the sites that were affected—they really liked that article and they were happy to see themselves in there, plus it got picked up by national television news which gets distributed all over the world so they were really happy. Unfortunately, it had to be a disaster to get them in there." Underneath Diane's professional aura was a very caring person.

The second outcome observed in the entrepreneurial journeys of all four women was the issue of profitability. This particular outcome delineated the differences between the shopkeepers and the home-businesswomen. Amy, a shopkeeper, got into the business "for the people and the love of it. Unfortunately...I have to think about finances." Later she said, "I am hoping it will become, well, profitable." Barbara, the second shopkeeper, admitted that she had been offered a position that would have meant a better income when she was in the midst of opening her store, yet she was willing to wait for the profits to come. Three years later, without a lot of profitability she divulges, "I think happiness and the money go hand in hand...if you are not making money, the fun kind of goes away after awhile."

On the other hand, Diane and Sandi, the home businesswomen, did not dwell on profitability. Sandi honestly confided, "With regard to the dollar, ask me how much money I made last year. I would not know..." When she won the annual sales award, she reiterated, "You are given a forecast and a budget." Somehow she won the award, which included a bonus. Yet "it wasn't the dollar that drew me to that job." It was the contacts for her consulting company that drew her toward selling. She did not think money should be uppermost in her thoughts. Diane seemed to share Sandi's response to money. She hinted that she would not quit even if she did have lots of money. "If I won the lottery, I'd accept the $10 million, but there are some clients I wouldn't keep."

Sustainability was the last contextual theme that proved important to continuing the experience. Sustainability referred to the psychological and sociological elements that affected the entrepreneur's decision to continue the journey. Amy, Barbara, Diane, and Sandi all introduced the first issue of sustainability, that of balance between home and the workplace. The second issue, moral support for the journey, proved interesting because it differed amongst the four women. In addition, the desire to continue with the specific entrepreneurial journey proved to be surprising, since each one had indicated their pleasure at being interviewed as successful entrepreneurs when first contacted.

All of them indicated that they experienced difficulty in achieving equilibrium between work and home, yet recognized that balance was necessary for sustaining their respective journeys. Amy admitted that finding a balance between home and work has been nearly impossible. She believes more is expected of the working mother than the father is in her generation but feels this attitude will improve with the next generation. When asked if the job had to come first, Amy answered, "Yes…It has to come first." She began her journey with the idea of keeping home and business separated, but to no avail. She takes being a mother and a manager seriously, and trying to maintain a balance is difficult. "I do have high expectations and that is probably in all honesty my downfall too. My expectations are very high. 100% on everything…so I am learning to cope with that."

Barbara also emphasized achieving equilibrium between home and business. She stressed, "I think it is so important to really balance your life, and work can become everything." She warned, "When you are an entrepreneur obviously you have workaholic tendencies that can take over." To prevent the business from taking over her personal life completely, she opted to close the shop on Sundays so she could relax with her partner.

Like Barbara, Sandi made time for both herself and her family. But she did not always think that way. Before being fired, she told me, "80% of my life was involved in work, 5% was my kids, 3% was my husband, and 2% was me. So when I lost 80% of my life I had no residual". The entrepreneurial course she enrolled in prior to beginning her journey focussed on "setting goals and being balanced—being a more balanced person.

What buys you a sort of happy life is being balanced." Three years after taking the entrepreneurial course, she could tell me, "my priority is my children." As a divorced woman, she had begun taking individual vacations with each of her three children. While she honestly divulged that "I am not as balanced as I'd like to be," she indicated that "The *Simple Abundance* book just keeps reminding you every day of what is important in your life."

Although Diane had not taken an entrepreneurial course, she, too, said, "I think you have to strike a balance." She discussed balance in terms of internal and external obstacles. Like Barbara, her internal obstacle was dealing with the anxiety of running her business. When the workload seems too big she either sub-contracts it or breaks it into smaller projects so she does not feel so inundated with work. "If I am really busy I will force myself to take a break because I know you can't sit here for seven hours straight." She began every day with exercise and would allow herself time during the day to walk or bicycle. Diane described the external obstacles as "all the other stuff that sort of interferes with getting your work done, and that could be family things. You know you are going great guns and your child has to come home sick. You have to change gears because she needs you." Diane worked at solving these external problems. "I think the way around that is by doing some planning. For example, I try not to let the deadlines get so tight…I always leave some slack in the schedule." Diane's family was very much a priority. She referred to them throughout the conversation as part of the balancing act.

The four women all found ways of gaining support, but there were interesting ways of approaching it. Both Amy and Barbara had successful entrepreneurial parents, so for them, entrepreneurship was just a way of life. Amy knew she wanted to own her own shop and put it off until her children were a little older. As a single parent she is lucky to be able to depend on her parents for both child care and moral support in her entrepreneurial journey. Barbara mentioned, "In university I took entrepreneurship courses, which I don't know why; they interested me but obviously at that point I was even thinking of my own business then." Not only did Barbara have parental support, but she also had support from her husband. "My husband is a rock. Our personal life has always been very solid. Without that it would be hard to carry this on my own. He has been there—he is an experienced entrepreneur…He knows all the stuff and knows what to say to get me through it."

On the other hand, neither Sandi nor Diane had had a parent who modeled the entrepreneurial lifestyle, and neither received much support from anyone when they first indicated an interest in beginning an entrepreneurial journey. When Sandi started her consulting business, she was made to feel insignificant and unworthy of her consulting fees. In her depressed state she was often brought to tears at the onset of her journey. Finally one cosmetic surgeon proved to be supportive and hired her as a laser consultant.

Diane told her husband over dinner of her decision to become an entrepreneur. Unlike Sandi, Diane was much stronger in her decision. However, she added, "I don't think he was very supportive…But then when I actually started getting paid for writing he was saying, 'Oh gee, I guess there's something to this.'"

Both Barbara and Amy had entrepreneurial families who supported them from the beginning, which helped sustain them in their entrepreneurial experience. Neither Diane nor Sandi enjoyed such support, yet both of these women continued to sustain their journeys, without letting go of their dream.

Some surprising differences among the women emerged in relation to their desire to continue the journey. Amy reflected, "I am not sure that I will stay in this…I can't see myself in this in six years time, or four years time, possibly three years time. I think this had to be the most difficult thing I have every done in my life is open this store…I don't know if I would ever do it [franchise] again." She did soften these statements with, "I am really not sorry I have done this." But she added later, "You have to give up a lot. I didn't realize it at the time growing up. I do, looking back…You have to work for what you want." By the end of the interview, she decisively stated, "This year will be the deciding fact: do I continue or not?" Her final words indicated her decreasing desire to continue in her chosen journey: "If it feels wrong, get out!"

Barbara also debated whether she should continue her chosen entrepreneurial journey when she said, "If you have a good month, maybe you can take some time off…And you don't have a regular income. So those things are more important now than they were even 6 months ago to me." She indicated, "Your priorities shift…I'll always be a business person and probably have other ventures a couple of years down the line, even if I do work for somebody else for a few years. It will be sort of back and forth." She honestly admitted, "I don't have any kids and I have always been career minded. It has always been really clear for me." It has been 3 ½ years since she opened her store, which for Barbara, means it is time to do something different. "That is why now I am looking at making changes here and see what happens."

Diane, on the other hand, had had full time job offers, but said, "I wouldn't see why I would leave [the business]…I am just not interested. What would I do? You either work for someone else or not work at all. I can't afford to not work at all." Diane wanted to continue her entrepreneurial journey because she knew her clients were pleased with her work, which in turn proved satisfying. Sandi also indicated that she had had many outside opportunities. For example, "The collagen company offered me a job going internationally." She refused because she still has children at home. Instead she decided to concentrate on "developing my services by being good at what I do." She confided that when she worked for the hospital, "I was worried that I could lose my job." Now that she has her own business she wonders what she was so worried about. Sandi certainly was not thinking of discontinuing her journey because she was having a good time. She told me, "I enjoy it [the business] so much, and I don't worry anymore. I don't worry!"

As the individual begins and continues the journey, many aspects of the trip will be meaningful along the way. There is the potential to have a good trip or a bad trip, but, in either case, it will probably be significant in one way or another. Analogous to the meaningful aspects on a trip, there are the contextual elements of the entrepreneurial journey which create meaning for the new venturer. The impetus for beginning the journey, personal control, outcomes of the journey, and the sustainability of the journey will all provide significance to the entrepreneurial experience.

To End or not to End the Entrepreneurial Journey

The constellation of operational elements was how they "took care of business," and turned out to be the determining factor of whether they continued the entrepreneurial journey or terminated it. The most important components that emerged within the operational elements included hours of operation and need for employees, inventory, business site, and promotion of the business.

Hours of Operation and Need for Employees

The hours of operation and required help were different for the two groups of women. Amy's franchise dictated that her hours of operation were from 7:00 a.m. to 11:00 p.m. daily, including Sundays and holidays. She worked at building and motivating a great team. Initially when she opened the shop with 17 employees, "labour was 95% of our take per month." Eighteen months later labour was at about 20% with 11 employees. But she still must contend with paying overtime on statutory holidays and remaining open according to the franchise rules.

While Barbara set her own shop hours, she was open daily and at least one evening, although she did decide to close on Sundays and holidays. Like Amy, Barbara could not run the shop all those hours by herself. After a few problems finding good help, Barbara now has two dependable women working for her on a part-time basis.

Diane and Sandi had completely different circumstances. Sandi kept flexible hours during the week because she traveled as a sales representative. However, she was always available through her answering service and cellular phone. She had no employees. Diane had no staff either, and remarked, "I can't imagine that because I would have to move into an office and that's a whole other thing. And I don't see that happening." In theory, Diane's hours were 9:00 a.m. to 5:00 p.m. weekdays. However, she could be flexible because she could leave the office and let the answering machine take messages while she attended meetings or her children's functions. Alternatively, she may work on the weekend. "There is the odd time when that would happen, but not on a regular basis…If I'm really busy— there was a period last year where I would work every Saturday morning from 8 to 10." In short, because these women were single-employee home businesswomen, their work schedules were far more flexible and adaptive than were those of Amy and Barbara.

Inventory

The need for turning inventory varied according to the nature of the venture. Both shopkeepers Amy and Barbara had inventory to worry about. Barbara commented, "There are a lot of aspects to retail–you know, inventory being a large part of it. Managing inventory is a very tough thing for anybody. I talk to friends in manufacturing and they say that is probably the single most difficult part of business because you really have to kind of see the future to get the right mix." Barbara indicated how quickly an entrepreneur could get into trouble with suppliers. "Paying the suppliers on time–I was really diligent the first year and a half or so, but you get a little behind. You have one bad month–it really, really puts you behind." Barbara also indicated that even if she seemed to be making a lot of sales, she would be behind in paying suppliers. "It should not be a problem, but it seems to be." Unlike Barbara, Amy did not have 15 years in business, and she confided, "Honestly, it scares me because there is a lot of coffee being sold here to cover the expenses per month, but it is not enough. I don't know. I really don't know." She also realized, "You need a full year or even a year and a half to know what your fluctuations are going to be…You are going to know your real peak times and your dead times. And in those peak times you have to be able to pay as much as you can and store as much as you can so when dead times hit you've got cover. And I just learned that."

Alternatively, Sandi and Diane did not have to contend with inventory problems in their entrepreneurial journey. In fact, Diane questioned whether she could be defined as an entrepreneur since she believed that true entrepreneurs "take a chunk of money and invest it" in their business. "If it had not worked out I could have just gone to work for someone else and would have lost six month's or a year's salary." While Sandi did not have an option to work for someone else during the height of the recession when many nurses were being laid off, she also did not have to carry inventory. All she required was a small loan. "I needed $5,000. So what I did, I put in $2,500 and the bank put in $2,500 to buy office equipment." As a clinician she was paid consulting fees, and as a collagen sales representative, "I am only paid for the 2 days that I work…I'm working as an independent agent for this company." For Diane and Sandi, then, there was no worry about turning inventory in their home-based business, while for Amy and Barbara it was a constant concern to keep their shops well stocked.

Business Site

The cost of setting up and maintaining a separate business location from their home was an issue that only Amy and Barbara had to contend with from the outset of the entrepreneurial journey. Amy exclaimed, "A lot goes into these franchises. A lot of loans. Almost $400,000 to purchase this. And that doesn't include your inventory. It doesn't include your staff…Then you pay 11% to keep the name—per month." Although Barbara did not buy a franchise, she had to set up expensive displays in her rented space. She hired the women who sewed window coverings and soft furniture for her commercial clients to make samples for her shop. She defrayed display costs in some interesting ways, such as the photo album with pictures of window treatments. While Barbara had been in the same location for three years, she experienced numerous problems renegotiating her lease. "We just battled back and forth and ended up having a small increase."

Meanwhile, Sandi and Diane both worked from a home office. Diane turned a bedroom into an upstairs office. She equipped it with an excellent computer system, a fax machine, and an extra phone line. Meanwhile, Sandi spread her desk and computer equipment in separate areas of her basement. As a freelance consultant, Sandi simply walked into a well-designed clinic with superior equipment. There were beautifully appointed offices where she displayed her degree and certificates. In short, because these two businesswomen worked from the home they had little site cost in comparison to Barbara and Amy who had to rent shop space.

Promotion of the Business

The final point involved the way in which these two groups of entrepreneurs promoted their respective businesses. Amy and Barbara constantly advertised their enterprises to attract customers. Both women had a file filled with publicity. Amy advertised in diverse media. In addition, she said, "I couldn't keep track of all the functions I have joined...I think that is part of the community–a very costly thing."

Barbara mentioned changing her advertising from the local paper to a regional one. In addition, she sends out mailings to sports organizations she has joined, and has attended networking breakfasts.

Diane and Sandi had a different approach to promoting their entrepreneurial ventures. When Diane was asked how she moved her business forward, she had to ponder the answer. Her client satisfaction survey and newsletter were her main means. Sandi realized she had many opportunities due to the contacts she had in the business. Like Diane, Sandi handled most of her own promotion, with very little expense involved, compared to the two shopkeepers.

As the trip continues then there are specific details involved in travelling to a destination. For example, there are car rentals, airplane flights, hotel accommodations, meal reservations, and entertainment that must be attended to on the journey. Eventually the traveler may have to terminate the trip if unable to continue to attend to all of these needs. The entrepreneur must consider hours of operation, need for employees, inventory, business site, and promotion of the business. These are the crucial factors that may cause the new venturer to terminate the entrepreneurial journey if unable to meet the requirements due to stress, finances, or exhaustion.

Three Major Elements That Play A Role In The Entrepreneurial Journey

Elements	Characteristics
Personal Elements	
Skills	Technical Human Administrative
Attitudes	Drive Persistence Ambiguity
Personality Traits	Creative Innovative
Sociological Conditions	Gender Educational Background Age Childhood Background
Contextual Elements	
Impetus for Beginning Journey	"Pull" "Push"
Personal Control	Freedom of Choice
Outcome of Journey	Service Profitability
Sustainability of the Journey	Balance Moral Support Desire to Continue the Journey
Operational Elements	Hours of Operation Need for Employees Inventory Business Site Promotion of Business

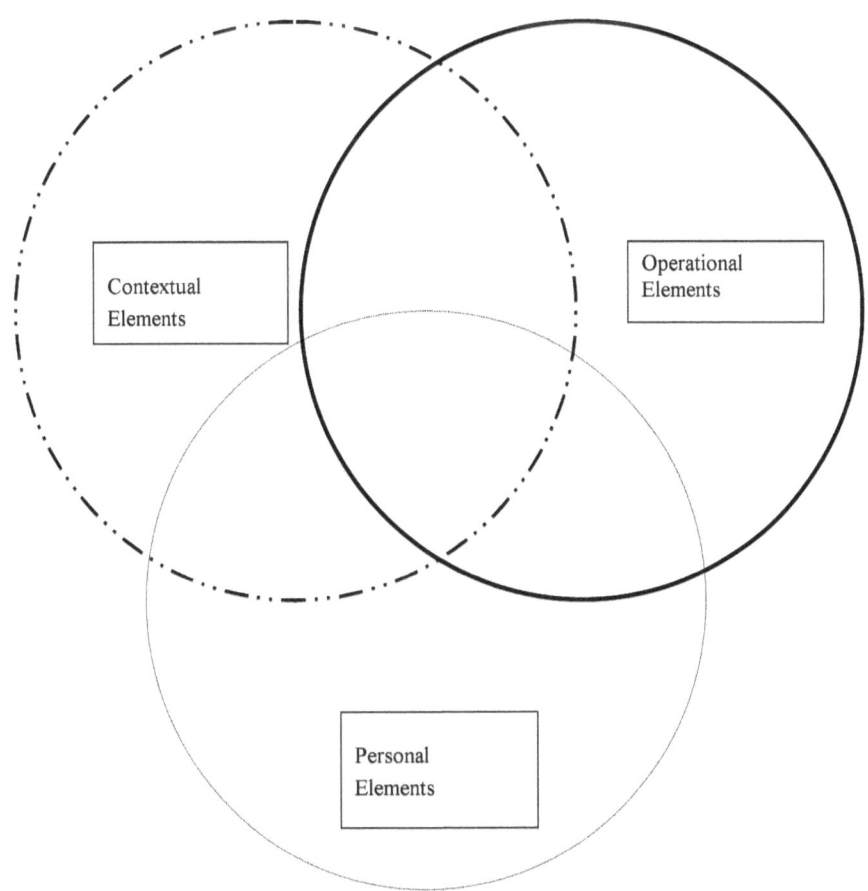

Integration of the Three Elements

CHAPTER SIX

▼

JOURNEY TO THE AUTHENTIC SELF: A HOLISTIC CONSTELLATION

Two distinct groups of entrepreneurial women generated many similarities and differences with respect to both personal and contextual elements of the journey. The most important similarity was balance. Both groups of entrepreneurs continually addressed the balance between the homefront and the workplace. Not surprisingly, however, the major differences amongst the four women in this study were divided in terms of the two groups. For shopkeepers Amy and Barbara, finding a balance proved to be stressful. They are not alone. In their book, *Work, Industry, and Canadian Society*, Krahn and Lowe report that, "when the Conference Board of Canada surveyed 11,000 employees across Canada in 1988-89, it discovered that two-thirds had some difficulty balancing work and family." Barbara admitted to having hit a low point the previous summer and still felt anxious that her personal life was suffering. Amy, a single parent, knew her family life had deteriorated, but felt she had to put the business first to continue her entrepreneurial journey. Krahn and Lowe also had something to say about this work-family conflict:

work has changed. Women have changed…This strain between the change in women and the absence of change in much else leads me to speak of a stalled revolution. Perhaps the most pervasive consequence of this stalled revolution is the rise of job-family conflict.

Both shopkeepers revealed their struggles as they attempted to find a balance between their domestic and professional lives.

On the other hand, Sandi and Diane seemed close to achieving a balance. As a single mother, Sandi took separate vacations with each of her three children, and, as an entrepreneur, had an excellent working relationship with both the clinic and the collagen company. Diane had trained her children not to interrupt her while in her home office, yet she let the answering service take any calls when she had a function to attend with her children. Diane and Sandi seemed to confirm Schwarz's observation in his book, *Breaking With Tradition: Women and Work, The New Facts of Life*:

Social change, driven by demography, education, and prosperity, begets value change…The baby boomers and women bring new values and attitudes about work, family life, and society to…business. The new value shift centers around time, quality, self-fulfillment, children, and general satisfaction with life.

As they continued on their journey, Sandi and Diane seemed to have achieved a balance between their personal and business lives by establishing specific values and working to maintain them.

Clearly all four women had multiple roles, but, again, Sandi and Diane seemed to move between the roles more easily than Amy and Barbara. In her book, *The Female Advantage: Women's Ways of Leadership*, Helgesen touches on this notion of multiple roles when she discusses the business leaders, who

viewed their jobs as just one element of who they were. Other aspects of their lives simply took up too much time to permit total identification with their careers. "Raising two kids alone, how could I forget that I'm a mom and a manager?" asked [one entrepreneur].

One of Helgesen's entrepreneurs summed it up: "It's not as if I'm different people. I'm just playing up different parts of who I am." These four women certainly discussed the idea of being more than the owner of a business. Sandi and Diane set timelines that they followed so they could do an excellent job for their clients while leaving time to enjoy life with their respective families. However, Barbara found that her job encroached more on her personal life than she had planned, while Amy seemed slightly overwhelmed by the daunting chore of having to be head of the household as well as head of the shop. Moving easily from one role to another while on the entrepreneurial journey proved more difficult for the shopkeepers than for the other two women.

A critical skill that emerged was the ability to multi-task. All four entrepreneurs demonstrated their ability to handle more than one job at a time. Amy could clean tables while carrying on a conversation with several customers at a time, yet be aware of the need to run back to the counter to serve more customers. Barbara could continue to cut fabric for one customer while answering her portable phone, and then give advice to yet another customer on customized blinds. Diane shifted easily from writing a news bulletin for one client to writing a newsletter for another client while waiting for telephone calls to update information for the bulletin. Sandi froze one patient for collagen injections, chatted to another client about having laser treatment, and then moved on to discuss varicose veins with another patient, all within the matter of a very few minutes. All four of these businesswomen demonstrated amazing capability of juggling many jobs at once. It was their ability to multi-task that kept the four businesswomen functioning effectively on a daily basis.

As the journey continued for all four women, the inner workings of the enterprise clearly defined the division between the two groups. Details such as having employees, turning inventory, and maintaining a business site proved to be major roadblocks in Amy's and Barbara's journeys. Diane and Sandi, on the other hand, did not contend with any of these operational costs. Amy's 11 part-time staff drained her profits, especially when statutory holidays dictated overtime salaries. Barbara's major staffing problem was finding qualified personnel who could sell the merchandise; this took its toll on her personally. In short, only the shopkeepers had to contend with the expenses and the difficulties of hiring good employees. Williamson, in his book, *Your Guide to Starting and Self-financing Your Own Business In Canada*, says, "inventory is like cash. Make sure it works for you!" Both Amy and Barbara were trying to maintain their inventory, but not without experiencing some cash flow problems. In bad months, such as January for Amy and February for Barbara, sales did not equal the accounts payable. In summary, only the shopkeepers had to contend with the worry, the hardship, and the expense of carrying inventory.

Furthermore, Williamson states that "overheads can certainly be reduced by working out of your home or apartment." While Amy's franchise dictated where her business site was located, Barbara had chosen her own site away from home. Both women watched much of their profits go into continuing their entrepreneurial journey just in the location alone. The shopkeepers had to cut into their profits to pay for a business site.

For the two shopkeepers, then, having to contend with employees, inventory and a business site was proving detrimental to their venture. Indeed, is it any wonder that both of them considered the possibility of terminating the journey? For Amy and Barbara, it just might not be feasible to continue the journey.

All four women strived to do and be the best that they could be as entrepreneurs and as productive, caring members of society. Each of them shared their struggles and their joys as they dealt with the combination of integrated elements on their respective journeys. Amy and Barbara even admitted that they were considering terminating their journeys because of the inherent operational components. Yet all four of these businesswomen provided hope for women who want careers in entrepreneurship. None of them was without hope. They all discussed the experience in terms of learning and growing as people on an entrepreneurial journey that was part of a holistic life journey.

In *The Road Less Traveled*, psychiatrist Scott Peck discussed this holistic life journey in terms of achieving a high level of self-understanding. Peck made no distinction between achieving spiritual growth and mental growth. Amy, Barbara, Diane, and Sandi were also trying to achieve a high level of self-understanding as they grew mentally in their capacity as new venturers. In *The Re-Enchantment of Everyday Life*, psychologist Thomas Moore suggested applying the principles of caring for the soul to our everyday environment. Amy, Barbara, Diane, and Sandi did try to care for their customers, their families, and their own souls as they continued their entrepreneurial journey daily.

Perhaps Sarah Ban Breathnach's book, *Simple Abundance*, captures the heart of what each of these women was trying to achieve in her own entrepreneurial journey, that is, to find her authentic self. Sandi referenced Ban Breathnach's book when she described her personal journey from a frightened, depressed, unemployed woman to a confident, joyful entrepreneurial woman. Diane talked about having to become a writer so she "didn't miss the boat," that is, she found this was her life's work. Amy and Barbara may terminate their journeys, but they have learned a lot about their authentic selves. Barbara knew she thrived on spending more time with her husband and family, while Amy knew she needed to work with people. All four women seemed to discover that entrepreneurship was a path on the journey of life that helped them find their authentic selves.

EPILOGUE

▼

When I last spoke to each of these women, every one was still running their own business and making a profit. I salute each of them as they continue their respective journeys.

About the Author

▼

Darlene E. Jones has written articles for newspapers and educational journals. As a training and development specialist, Darlene writes this first book from a solid research base in small business. This Canadian author welcomes critical response as she continues her study and investigation of other current business and general interest topics. Feedback may be submitted to *djones25@home.com*